"Andrea Celenza explores in this seminal book one of the most difficult – and not surprisingly least visited – theoretical/clinical areas of psychoanalysis from its beginnings to the present. With her long specific experience in observing and treating these often highly problematic transference configurations, she succeeds in clearly describing their variety and complexity. Erotic transference is thus transformed, in many cases, from insurmountable obstacles to treatment into valuable opportunities for ever deeper and more effective analysis at the heart of human sometimes dramatic relational experience."

Stefano Bolognini, MD, IPA Past-President, author of
Vital Flows between Self and Non-Self: The Interpsychic
(Routledge, 2022)

"Erotic transferences are ubiquitous. However, they are often denied, buried, projected, dismissed, overlooked, feared, or hidden in the darkest corners of the psyche. In this outstanding tour de force, Andrea Celenza brings them out of the darkness and into the daylight. In so doing, she enlightens her readers while also providing the reader with a brilliant guide. I highly recommend it to clinicians and educators alike."

Glen O. Gabbard, MD, Clinical Professor of Psychiatry,
Baylor College of Medicine, author of *Boundaries and
Boundary Violations in Psychoanalysis* (American
Psychiatric Publishing, 2016)

"I thought I knew a lot about this topic, but I learned many new things from this lucid, accessible, and stimulating book. Andrea Celenza is right that psychoanalysis has been desexualized. As one of the foremost experts on sexual misconduct, she now places that phenomenon in the much larger and more positive context of the erotic dimensions of psychotherapy. What she writes will be essential reading for therapists of all schools and at all levels of experience."

Prof. Andrew Samuels, author of *A New Therapy for
Politics?* (Routledge, 2019) and *From Sexual Misconduct to
Social Justice* (Psychoanalytic Dialogues, 1996)

Erotic Transferences

Erotic Transferences: A Contemporary Introduction offers a comprehensive introduction to this key, yet challenging aspect of the psychoanalytic process.

Despite emerging frequently in the psychoanalytic process, Andrea Celenza highlights the sparseness of literature on erotic transferences and a tendency to desexualize psychoanalytic theorizing, which she posits is a result of the inherent threat erotic transferences can pose to the analyst. By providing a thorough overview of the topic, clarifying terminology, and providing vivid case examples, Celenza seeks to redress this omission. Throughout this volume, she discusses the interplay of power and gender, along with chapters on the temptation of disclosure and the disturbing prevalence of sexual boundary violations.

Providing practitioners with the tools to deal with the intense feelings that inevitably arise with erotic transferences, this book is vital reading for all psychoanalysts at all levels of experience and seniority, psychodynamic practitioners, instructors, candidates, and trainees.

Andrea Celenza, PhD, is a Training and Supervising Analyst at the Boston Psychoanalytic Society and Institute and Assistant Clinical Professor at Harvard Medical School. She is also Adjunct Faculty at the NYU Post-Doctoral Program in Psychoanalysis and The Florida Psychoanalytic Center. She has written over 60 papers and three books on love, sexuality, and psychoanalysis. The recipient of several awards, her writings have been translated into Italian, Spanish, Korean, Russian and Farsi. Her third book, entitled, *Transference, Love, Being: Essential Essays from the Field*, was published in 2022 by Routledge.

Routledge Introductions to Contemporary Psychoanalysis

Aner Govrin, Ph.D.
Series Editor
Yael Peri Herzovich, Ph.D.
Executive Editor
Itamar Ezer
Assistant Editor

"Routledge Introductions to Contemporary Psychoanalysis" is one of the prominent psychoanalytic publishing ventures of our day. It will comprise dozens of books that will serve as concise introductions dedicated to influential concepts, theories, leading figures, and techniques in psychoanalysis covering every important aspect of psychoanalysis. The length of each book is fixed at 40,000 words.

The series' books are designed to be easily accessible to provide informative answers in various areas of psychoanalytic thought. Each book will provide updated ideas on topics relevant to contemporary psychoanalysis – from the unconscious and dreams, projective identification and eating disorders, through neuropsychoanalysis, colonialism, and spiritual-sensitive psychoanalysis. Books will also be dedicated to prominent figures in the field, such as Melanie Klein, Jaque Lacan, Sandor Ferenczi, Otto Kernberg, and Michael Eigen.

Not serving solely as an introduction for beginners, the purpose of the series is to offer compendia of information on particular topics within different psychoanalytic schools. We ask authors to review a topic but also address the readers with their own personal views and contribution to the specific chosen field. These books will make intricate ideas comprehensible without compromising their complexity.

We aim to make contemporary psychoanalysis more accessible to both clinicians and the general educated public.

Aner Govrin - Editor

Erotic Transferences
A Contemporary Introduction
Andrea Celenza

For more information about this series, please visit: www.routledge.com/ Routledge-Introductions-to-Contemporary-Psychoanalysis/book-series/ ICP

Erotic Transferences

A Contemporary Introduction

Andrea Celenza

Routledge
Taylor & Francis Group

LONDON AND NEW YORK

Designed cover image: © Michal Heiman, Asylum 1855–2020,
The Sleeper (video, psychoanalytic sofa and Plate 34),
exhibition view, Herzliya Museum of Contemporary Art, 2017

First published 2025
by Routledge
4 Park Square, Milton Park, Abingdon, Oxon OX14 4RN

and by Routledge
605 Third Avenue, New York, NY 10158

Routledge is an imprint of the Taylor & Francis Group, an informa business

British Library Cataloguing-in-Publication Data
A catalogue record for this book is available from the British Library

ISBN: 9781032488325 (hbk)
ISBN: 9781032471068 (pbk)
ISBN: 9781003391012 (ebk)

DOI: 10.4324/9781003391012

Typeset in Times New Roman
by codeMantra

Contents

Preface

This series of introductory texts aspires to cover the full spectrum of essential topics and authors in psychoanalysis, along with the hope of addressing gaps in our literature. There is a deep void surrounding the topic of erotic transferences, extant throughout the history of psychoanalysis despite that all practitioners struggle with this most important, commonly occurring clinical challenge. In this volume, I propose that the paucity of literature on this subject results from a chronic *desexualization* of our theorizing. I describe this desexualization over the historical arc of psychoanalytic theorizing in the Introduction. I also suggest that this desexualization is reflective of the acute threat posed by this complex, indeed risky topic.

This volume covers the wide expanse of erotic transferences and their various manifestations, beginning with the clarification of important *terminology* (Chapter 2). Using a quasi-developmental infrastructure, including case illustrations with both female and male analysands, I begin with early *maternal erotic transferences* (Chapter 3). In this chapter, I rely on Object-Relational, Attachment, and Relational approaches to explicate how these transferences reveal themselves. The next chapter follows these two cases as the analyses flourished and evolved into *oedipal-level erotic transferences* (Chapter 4). I describe the strands of aggression and envy that form their building blocks and various meanings, primarily viewed through a neo-Kleinian lens. Finally, the topic of *gender* itself is discussed in Chapter 5 where a maternal erotic transference is differently conceived through a neo-Classical lens. The last two chapters discuss the ever-present difficulties with containment and temptations of *erotic language and feelings* as well as the ubiquitous and persistent problem of *sexual boundary violations* (Chapters 6 and 7, respectively).

Epistemologically, I take an intersubjective, social-constructivist approach and, therefore, describe clinical manifestations that reflect this underlying foundation. On a clinical level, I take seriously all of the psychoanalytic approaches to emergent phenomena, including neo-Classical, neo-Kleinian, Object-Relational, Relational, and Post-Bionian Field Theoretical systems. The latter especially permeates my understandings of the role of countertransferences as this vantage point provides an essential channel for unconscious communication. All of these perspectives are organically interwoven into the pertinent case illustrations.

This series will be an extremely valuable resource for instructors and practitioners alike, especially in those areas, such as erotic transferences, where practitioners feel insufficiently guided and prepared for what might emerge. I am honored to be a part of this project.

Acknowledgments

I am indebted to all my patients, necessarily anonymous, for their courage and openness throughout the analytic process. I thank them for trusting me and helping us understand the intensity of feelings with which we struggled together.

I am grateful to the publishing companies for permission to excerpt and/or reprint from the following papers or chapters:

Journal of the American Psychoanalytic Association: Celenza, A. (2006). The threat of male-to-female erotic transference, 54(4): 1207–1231. https://doi.org/10.1177/00030651060540040401

Journal of the American Psychoanalytic Association: Celenza, A. (2022). Maternal erotic transferences and the work of the abject, 70(1):9–38. https://doi.org/10.1177/00030651221084595

Psychoanalysis and #MeToo: Where are we in this movement? by Andrea Celenza (2022). *International Journal of Controversial Discussions*, 2(1):48–71.

The guilty pleasure of erotic transferences: Searching for radial true, by Andrea Celenza (2010). *Studies in Gender and Sexuality*, reprinted by permission of Informa UK Limited, trading as Taylor & Francis Group, www.tandfonline.com.

Copyright 2022 from *Forward* by Andrea Celenza, In *Braving the Erotic Field in the Psychoanalytic Treatment of Children and Adolescents* by Mary T. Brady (Ed.). Reproduced by permission of Taylor and Francis Group, LLC, a division of Informa pic.

Transference, Love, Being: Essential Essays from the Field by Andrea Celenza. Copyright 2022, by Imprint. Reproduced by permission of Taylor and Francis Group, LLC, a division of Informa pic.

Erotic Revelations: Clinical Applications and Perverse Scenarios by
Andrea Celenza. Copyright 2014, by Imprint. Reproduced by permission of Taylor and Francis Group, LLC, a division of Informa pic.

*Sexual Boundary Violations: Therapeutic, Supervisory and Aca-
demic Contexts,* [Chapter 1] by Andrea Celenza. Copyright 2007,
2011, Reproduced by permission of Jason Aronson, Inc., Rowman
& Littlefield Publishing Group.

Rivista di Psicoanalisi: Celenza, A. (2013). Transfert erotici materni
e desideri di fusion (Maternal erotic transferences and merger
wishes), LIX(4):821–838.

Chapter 1

Introduction

The place of sexuality and eroticism in psychoanalysis is like the lost city of Atlantis, shrouded in mystery, fantastic, and ideal, yet uncannily disappeared and dismissed (as if) lacking in evidence. Despite that psychoanalysis was founded, then elaborated on this fundamental drive (Freud being our Plato), the dimensions of Eros are eternally evanescent, ultimately erased in our discourse, found and refound along the way only to be lost again. Now is a time of its reemergence, yet even in current day practice there is a constant shying away.

A legend of an ideal city, Atlantis was first described in Plato's *Timaeus*.[1] The story is told through the words of Timaeus (a fictional Pythagorean philosopher from Southern Italy) to Socrates in a monologue on the creation of the world. He describes Atlantis as

> a vast power... that sprang forth from beyond, larger than Libya and Asia ... a great and marvelous royal power ... set out to enslave all ... reach[ing] a point of extreme peril ... [the entire] force sank below the earth all at once ... and disappeared ... now unnavigable and unexplorable.

The parallels to erotic life are apparent. Eroticism creates the world, internally structuring our histories and vision of externality. Its inherent affective power threatens enslavement, we risk extreme peril seeking its ideal, and it regularly disappears from view.

The popular conception of Eros and the erotic qualities of life are typically associated with love and sexuality. In ancient mythology, however, Eros is (directly and indirectly) associated with a complex and contradictory set of intense affective instincts and drives, beyond love and sexuality. A primeval god of Greek mythology, later tradition

DOI: 10.4324/9781003391012-1

made Eros the son of Aphrodite, goddess of sexual love and beauty, with his father as either Zeus, (the king of gods), Ares (god of war and of battle), or Hermés (divine messenger of the gods).[2] Eros is the god of *passion*; passion defined as the sufferance or submission to intense feeling (i.e., love *and hate*).

The erotic in psychoanalytic theorizing and maternal eroticism is similarly complex. In his later work, Freud expanded his vision of the erotic to the broad life instincts. He wrote of an expanded vision of the sexual as early as 1910, where he acknowledged as belonging to "sexual life all expressions of tender feeling, we prefer to speak of *psychosexuality* .... Sexuality in the comprehensive sense: lieben (to love)" (p. 91, italics in original).

In the words of Merleau-Ponty (2012/1945), "The sexual is not the genital. It is what causes [one] to have a history ... provides a key to one's life." And further, "The body of the other is not perceived as an object, but rather as inhabited by a secret perception, by a sexual schema that is strictly individual ... the body [of the other] is enigmatic." Thus, we see Eros ignites life and we also see that with every desire comes a dread, a threat to one's being and very existence, because to encounter the other is to encounter *a mystery*. The mystery of the unknown, the challenge of separateness and difference, and the threat of the other's intentionality. Rilke (1939) warns of beauty, as "nothing but the beginning of terror .... That we revere it so because it calmly disdains to destroy us." Larger than Libya and Asia, indeed.

Desexualization of psychoanalytic theorizing

Given Freud's placement of sexuality in the center of his theorizing, the desexualization of psychoanalytic theorizing is especially surprising. Since his discovery of infantile sexuality and the establishment of the erotic instinct as fundamental to human nature, there has been a constant backing away. There is something about the inherent nature of sexuality that arouses fear and anxiety. It is not solely a contemporary phenomenon and yet it is only in the past several decades that papers focusing on the centrality of sexuality have emerged in our literature (Laplanche, 1989, 1997; Green, 1995; Fonagy, 2008; de Masi, 2012; Celenza, 2014; Atlas, 2016; Elise, 2019, to name a few authors). Interestingly, this desexualization is not solely the province of psychoanalysis, but goes back to ancient times in other fields. It is rooted in a tendency toward dualism that long predates Descartes, derived from a desire to transcend the body – to segregate and idealize pure reason and linear, abstract thought.

This dualism arises inevitably from fearing sexuality itself, not only because we are afraid of incest (as in sexual boundary violations) but because sexuality is inherently threatening. We resist erotic transferences and erotic countertransferences because we resist the exposure of narcissistic, oedipal-level wounds, our patient's as well as our own. Psychoanalytic authors (Klein, 1930; Britton, 1992) have written about the epistemophilic impulse and its inhibition due to traumatic experiences revolving around a child's curiosity of the primal scene. But perhaps most threatening is the mysterious other … sexuality is transgressive – we cross the boundaries of the unknown and penetrate a new frontier. Our vulnerability *is* our body, our nakedness, our desires in the face of the unknown other.

During Freud's era, the dualism in mind/body questions was in the zeitgeist. For Freud, this was about how the psyche needs to defend itself against inner forces to maintain stability. By 1905, Freud stated that we cannot know the contents of the unconscious and yet, he was also convinced that the mind was rooted in the body. How to contend with human reason and animal passion became his constant concern.[3]

In accord with the dual nature of inherent drives, sexuality is one force that structures human nature. In this way, the unconscious is rooted in sexuality (vitality and creativity) and in aggression (destructiveness). Yet we tend to interpret away from sexuality due to its inherent threatening nature, the fear of the mystery of the other, our ambivalence with regard to genital aims, and fears of loss of control.

Freud's era spanned the 1890s to the 1930s. This maps onto the Georgian, Victorian, and Edwardian eras in England, where there pervaded an intense religiosity and moralism. Freud himself faced great resistance to his formulations of libido and the sexual drive as basic to human nature. Yet he persevered,

> The psychoanalyst knows that the forces he works with are of the most explosive kind and that he needs as much caution and conscientiousness as a chemist. But when has it ever been forbidden to a chemist, on account of its danger, to occupy himself with the explosives which, just because of their effectiveness, are so indispensable?

(1915a, pp. 170–171)

We could wonder too if Freud's (1915a) straddling of the real/unreal ways of understanding transference love was another desexualizing move. Rather than forthrightly defining transference as *a shaping structure that signifies realness*,[4] Freud instructed analysts to "keep firm hold of the transference-love, but treat it as something unreal" (p. 166). A halfway backing away!

Then there emerged the scientism of the Enlightenment era, a scientism that determined to take the 'other' out of the field of observation. This structured our initial vision of the psychoanalytic enterprise – an essentially one-person psychology. The desexualization inherent in this is obvious. Freud himself expanded his interest in the erotic to the life instincts (1920, as reflected in *Beyond the Pleasure Principle*) to oppose Eros with Thanatos (the death instinct) and in this way, he changed his interest from the sexual instinct to the life and death instincts. Then Klein followed with her emphasis on aggression, destruction, the death drive, and object relations theorizing where pleasure and unpleasure became dominated by the defense of splitting and objects as good or bad. This was roughly in the 1930s to the 1960s in psychoanalytic theorizing.

Winnicott (1960) soon followed with his emphasis on the facilitating environment and the role of the mother as a holding function. Lacking erotic stimulus, development was conceived as provided and protected through containment. Birth and existence thus remained desexualized and deaggressivized. The 1970s and 1980s in psychoanalytic theorizing can be characterized by interest in the external object, trauma, separateness, and difference – once again, a deintensification of *instinctuality* in general. I propose that much of this deintensification of psychoanalytic theorizing arose from a fundamental fear of the other and a backing away from genital aims with their concomitant fears of loss of control, otherness, and desire in general.

With the era of relational theorizing, largely centered in America in the 1980s, there became a burgeoning (and much needed) interest in the maternal transferences. This was intertwined with infant observation studies and attachment theory, but through de-eroticized conceptions. As André Green (1995) stated, it is as if the etiologic determinants of psychopathology are thought to be located "before" or "beyond" sexuality. Muriel Dimen (1999) has attributed this desexualization in psychoanalysis to the paradigm shift in contemporary theory from drive to object relations, noting that "Where libido was, there shall objects be" (p. 417). We should not overlook the (unconscious?) substitution of 'objects' for 'others' (another desexualization through objectification) that remains everyday jargon in our literature. Fonagy (2008) quantified the apparent decline in interest in sexuality by examining word usage in electronically searchable journals of psychoanalysis. He found that the decline in *sexual* word usage is inversely related to the rise in *relational* word usage.

Eros in the clinical context

The desexualization of psychoanalytic theorizing continues to perplex and remains a missing aspect of the treatment situation as our anxieties and unconscious prohibitions inevitably move us away from erotics. This, despite that the clinical situation is an intimate relationship that easily lends itself to sexual metaphor. As I have written elsewhere (Celenza, 2014), the dialectic between holding and penetration fosters a mutual deepening as intimacy deepens – knowing the other is dialectically related to desiring the other; a mutual enhancement, one seemingly defining the other through opposition yet each paradoxically intensifying the other. To hold is to grasp; to penetrate is to transgress. Our work is penetrating and enveloping, incisive, and containing, a firm receptivity that retains, envelops, and holds the other in mind. The word *is* the touch is the affect is the knowledge.

Recalling Freud, *lieben* is to love. I put before us, as it were, the prospect of loving our patients and feeling sexually aroused … or not. The prospect of our full receptivity, in reverie, honed, and not denied. In the same anti-dualistic thinking, Hans Loewald, wrote in 1970 from *Psychoanalytic Theory and the Psychoanalytic Process*:

> Scientific detachment in its genuine form, far from excluding love is based on it. In our work it can be truly said that in our best moments of dispassionate and objective analyzing we love our object, the patient, more than at any other time and are compassionate with his whole being. In our field, scientific spirit and care for the object certainly are not opposites; they flow from the same source.
>
> (p. 65)

In clinical work, erotic erasure can be easily seen in contemporary theorizing of maternal transferences, reflected in the tendency to interpret downward (down and away, so to speak) from oedipal to preoedipal conceptualizations of sexuality,[5] resulting in a desexualization of the maternal erotic transference. There has been a tendency to interpret away from oedipal erotics toward a de-erotized maternal, to avoid the intensity of erotic transferences at both the oedipal level and within the maternal transferences. Contemporary writings that correct this erasure include the works of Chasseguet-Smirgel (1970), McDougall (1992), Balsam (2001, 2003, 2008, 2012, 2019), Benjamin (1995), Dimen (2003), Wrye and Welles (1994), Salomonsson (2012), Elise (2002, 2015, 2019), Celenza (2014, 2017, 2022a, 2022b), and Atlas (2016).

We must always be aware of the threat associated with erotic transferences and the tendency to mute or bias our focus. Perhaps we fear the mystery of the other and the intensity of what may arise. At the same time, we are lured to the erotic, as we want to unmask the mysteries of the others' being.

There is an amusing story of two friends in a nudist colony. They are walking, naked, together around the grounds. One has a band-aid on his upper arm. The other asks, "Can I see what's under that band-aid?" We are drawn to the hidden and mysterious; we are tempted to push boundaries, even in the most permissive contexts. What is the nature of this push, this urge to get beyond the immediate and inside the other? What are we looking for, what does it feel like? These are some of the questions that pertain to the present exploration into erotic life in the psychoanalytic and psychotherapeutic situation.

Far from Victorian England, Western cultures have made erotic life their plaything – we are bombarded with sexual imagery in all forms of media and entertainment – but do we understand it? Most importantly, can we *feel* it? I suspect the bombardment has had the opposite effect to what was intended – sexual imagery in the media is not necessarily a turn-on, but has become anesthetic.

Analysts must not be afraid to ask the question (always in our analysands' minds), Why can't we be lovers? This is an extension of Searles' writings in treating severely disturbed patients where he wisely said there needs to come a time in all treatments where the analyst can imagine marrying the patient.

We want our analyses to be thoroughgoing, to explore the full range of affects in all its intensity. This is our definition of health and refers to the absence of inhibition. In this effort, we must welcome whatever our patients bring. It is an affirmative attitude as the basis of non-judgmentalism, the contemporary version of neutrality. In order to do this, we have to be able to bear intense hatred, contempt, devaluing, rage, and envy in order to bring these affects to the fore so that our patients can deepen their self-understanding and self-acceptance. We must recognize as well the absence of sexual feeling for our patients, not as an easy path to abstinence or neutrality but as a *present absence*, a lack in our patient's vitality. In this way, our patients come to terms with, reckon with, and can take responsibility for their choices and lives. This is what we mean by wholeness and integration.

At the other end of the developmental continuum, erotic and loving transferences are not acknowledged either, especially in the final phases of a successful psychoanalysis and here I am referring to Bolognini's (1994) loving transference and affectionate transference. He describes erotic transferences along a continuum (from erotized, to erotic, to loving, and affectionate), comprising a broader range of meanings for erotic transferences.[6] I see Bolognini's attempt here not to delineate variations along the dimension of real/unreal but rather mature and less mature forms of attachment and love. In later years, he emphasized the need for the analyst to 'wear many hats' and to balance the need for recognition of sexuality with parental protectiveness (Bolognini, 2011).

Concluding remarks

In a general way, it has been said that psychoanalysis is all about sex; except for sex – that's about aggression. Always hidden, always deemed to be about something else! Further, there is confusion along another axis entirely – is it real or is it transference (i.e., unreal)? In this volume, I aim to put sexuality and eroticism back into psychoanalytic theorizing in both early formulations (as in the maternal erotic) and to delineate a place for pure erotic longing, along with the illustration of the variety of forms of homo-erotic and hetero-erotic desires. The framework of felt-experience (embodiment), multiplicity, and fluidity in gender theory will be employed to propose ways in which binarial constraints (e.g., feminine and masculine, so often interwoven with sexual concerns and inhibitions) may be transcended.

We now theoretically accept sexuality as fundamental to the structure of the mind (Green, 1995; Laplanche, 1989, 1997). For example, Laplanche's (1997, 1999) general theory of seduction depicts the mother as the universal driving force of all scenes of seduction, presenting the infant with her enigmatic, sexual unconscious. The infant *takes in* and translates these mysterious messages, constituting its unconscious. These affects and longings are then rekindled in later genital sexuality yet retain the maternal-infant dyad to serve as their template.

Despite these considerations, the metapsychological theorizing continues to be hidden, submerged, or lost when discussing clinical work. Now that countertransference is legitimated, viewed as a critical channel for unconscious communication, can erotic countertransference enter our discourse, i.e., the embodied and sexual analyst? One might ask how it might be possible to do treatment without the analyst's embodiment. Sterilized exploration suffers from constriction.... making the term 'erotic insufficiency' (Brady, 2022) particularly evocative of this missing dimension.

As analysts, we are the objects that will not be had, upholding the incest taboo and thereby cultivating a setting where early forms of desire can safely emerge. We must have the full range of affectivity at our disposal, but we must also help our patients reckon with, interpret, and be unafraid to experience the excitements and mysteries of their own bodies and the unknown other. At the same time, it behooves us to maintain awareness of the analyst's multiple roles in relation to the analysand, a multi-dimensional responsibility that is part of what should ultimately limit sexual boundary violations (see Modell, 1990; Bolognini, 2011; Celenza, 2014).

We don't go willingly into this terrain, for fear of its power, our own vulnerability in relation to it, the helplessness, excitement, and ignitability surrounding it. What if he says …? What if she wants…? What would I say? What will he feel? What might I *do*? It is crucial to remember that a *craving for love within the analytic setting is a demand for love in the absence of a capacity for loving.* Indeed, it is a manifestation of the reason a person seeks help.

There is also something inherent in sexuality that leads to a disclaiming, a dissociation, and a tendency to bury this vital spark of our humanity. When Freud began his journey into the creation of psychoanalytic methodology and theorizing, his first patients were female hysterics, those patients whose symptoms mimicked neurological disorders (especially the abnormal electrical firing of neurons culminating in seizures). Are we to ignore the associations of *fire* and *orgasmic-like* seizures? These experiences led Freud to wonder about the etiology of the symptomatic picture in these otherwise neurologically healthy women. He speculated that dissociated ideas were leading to abnormal behaviors and realized that the unconscious can take hold of the body.

For our purposes here, we should notice the dissociation of the affective component, the draining of the symptoms of their energy, their vitality, *their essence*.

Varied communities approach the conundrum and threat of sexuality differently or for different reasons, but the results tend to be the same. A muting, a deadening, a disclaiming, or discounting to reduce its power. The scientific community (of the Enlightenment era) endeavors to objectify subjectivity in order to measure it and thereby control its force. Religious communities tend to relegate sexuality to prohibited, if not sinful, arenas. Ethno-cultural communities tend to segregate these instincts as well, sometimes attributing the excesses of sexuality to demeaned subgroups or even genders. All this in order to disclaim our very humanity.

Freud (1917) too found the need to contend with objections to his preoccupation with sexuality, especially given that he placed it in the center of his theorizing:

> Opponents who do not understand the matter accuse us of one-sidedness and of overestimating the sexual instincts: 'Human beings have other interests besides sexual things.' We have not forgotten or denied this for a moment. Our one-sidedness is like that of the chemist who traces all compounds back to the force of chemical attraction. In doing so, he does not deny the force of gravity; he leaves that to the physicist to reckon with.
>
> (p. 349)

Our present-day scientism has replaced the blank screen of the Enlightenment era with a post-modern epistemology (essentially perspectivism). Transferences and countertransferences are now understood as a mutual construction, realities that are co-created. Yet we have to be comfortable. Our sexuality is aroused with the encounter of the other, the *mystery* of the other, our irreducible separateness, difference, and intentionality. There are always these unknown aspects. This is the nature of the threat.

This reminds me of an interaction I had with my analyst. One day, as I entered the office and crossed the room about to lie down, I saw, *to my horror*, a barrette on the couch. I took it between my fingers and held it up to him, asking, "You see other women?" To which he deftly responded, "It was a man wearing a wig." If only we all could respond with such deftness and aplomb, if not a touch of peskiness and teasing!

We have a large task ahead. We speak of things that resist revelation, surrounded with resistance, that don't want to be tamed while luring us to the edge, then disappear, leaving us empty-handed, bewildered, sometimes frightened, and yet always intrigued.

Notes

1 Cartwright, M. (2016). *World History Encyclopedia*. https://www.ancient.eu/atlantis/.
2 In the Theogony of Hesiod [c. 730–700 BC/2018].
3 See Makari (2008) for a thorough review of the historical climate and intellectual advances during Freud's time.
4 See Celenza (2022a, Essay 1, Transference, Real/Unreal) for more elaboration of these ideas.
5 I realize this assumes a linear developmental trajectory, which is problematic in itself.
6 Subsequently, Bolognini (2011) delineated multiple roles of the analyst in concordant relation to these transferences.

Chapter 2

What are erotic transferences?

Whenever I present or teach a seminar on erotic transferences, someone (with a note of panic in their voice) almost always asks, "But what do I do? What do I say? Just tell me that." To which I always respond, "Well, you have to know what is going on first." Erotic transferences are not one thing. They vary in structure and meaning, both of which will determine how to understand the phenomenon and what to say or interpret.

Before beginning our discussion of the complexity of these phenomena, we have to be clear about terminology. Given the dearth of writing in our literature on erotic transferences, there remains much confusion about terms, how they overlap, what they each delineate, and how to differentiate among them (Table 2.1).

First, *sexuality* refers to a range of *excitations* and activities that engender pleasure. These are not simply genital phenomena. The term refers to excitations that are fundamentally components of sexual love and arouse bodily pleasures. More specifically, the ***sexual instinct*** refers to sexual excitation that is bound to the functioning of any and all *erotogenic zones*. **Libido** is the *energy* associated with the sexual instinct. When we refer to ***sexualization***, we mean to denote the *defensive use* of sexual excitation to transform noxious experience into pleasure. It is a defensive response whose aim it is to transform unpleasurable experiences into pleasurable ones.

In a much more general sense, ***Eros*** refers to the *life instinct* (in contrast to the death instinct). Eros is *vitalization*, i.e., the energy that holds all living things together (binding). The term is derived from the Greek God of Passion (i.e., love and hate). Finally, when we call something ***erotic***, we mean to refer to the arousal of *sexual desire* or to refer

DOI: 10.4324/9781003391012-2

Table 2.1 Terminology

Sexuality – a range of excitations and activities that engender pleasure.

Sexual instinct – sexual excitation that is bound to the functioning of any and all erotogenic zones.

Libido – the energy associated with the sexual instinct.

Sexualization – the defensive use of sexual excitation to transform noxious experience into pleasure.

Eros – the life instinct (in contrast to the death instinct), vitalization, i.e., the energy that *holds all living things together* (binding).

Erotic – the arousal of sexual desire or referring to something as pertaining to sexual love, i.e., amatory, expressive of love, vitality, and life–giving feelings.

to something as pertaining to sexual love, i.e., amatory, expressive of love, vitality, and life-giving feelings.

From this terminology, we can see that the erotic and the sexual are intertwined with the experience and expression of love. As we know, Freud, discovered the phenomenon of transference by working with hysterical patients. These patients became more interested in a romantic relationship with him than discussing and addressing their symptomatology, the very reasons they sought help in the first place! As noted previously, we must always remember that the demand for love in the treatment context is *a demand for love in the absence of capacity for loving*. Therefore, we must not take this demand at face value. And we may be afraid of what lies behind it.

At the same time, erotic transferences are not always about love. They occur on a range, from healthy and affectionate (Bolognini, 1994) to sexualization as a defense against the full range of conflicts to the full variety of negative transferences. Indeed, *most erotic transferences are negative transferences* as we shall soon see. It is also imperative to attend to one's countertransference because there can be important communicative value in the meaning of what is being expressed in the analyst's countertransference and these conveyances have unconscious components. It may be that the only avenue to gain understanding of them is through our countertransference experience.

It is also important to remember that erotic urges can be used defensively by the analyst as well. Our literature reflects this. For most of the last century, our literature suggested that female analysts may mute the expression of urgent demands, especially by their male patients, interpreting downward (so to speak) in favor of a desexualized, maternal holding for fear of aggressive urges that may underlie erotic longings. This will be further discussed in the next chapter.

Types of erotic transferences

Here, I would like to introduce further clarification of terminology for ease of discussion. These terms relate to the expression of erotics and sexuality, all *expressed from within the transference* and are not terms outside of this context. A *sexualized transference* is comprised of the analysand's urgent demand to have sexual relations with the analyst. This is not necessarily an erotic relation and is characterized by a preoccupation with the sexual expression of need and desire. It is usually experienced simply and urgently, in a two-dimensional way, as if the need and action had little meaning. This is contrasted with the *introduction of erotics per se, which is the private imaginative use of the object of desire* (Bollas, 1994). An *erotic transference*, therefore, asks the question of *who we are* to our analysand in *their* imagined universe. Erotic transferences are the ways this imaginative use refers back to unresolved longings from the past but are now re-experienced in the present. Alternatively, erotic transferences may express newly emergent desires that the analysand is risking to express within the safe context of the treatment setting.

Therefore, the goal in treatment is first and foremost to *convert the sexualized transference into an erotic transference* in order to gain access to the analysand's fantasies. These then become the subject of analysis, including ubiquitous, fundamental questions that may exist in the analysand's mind such as, "Why can't we be lovers?" Another important and useful question to raise in the analyst's mind occurs when an erotic transference *does not* move the analyst, i.e., the absence of erotic desire in the pair. Why does this patient fail to arouse me?

The emergence of an erotic transference can be of many types. We can say now that the instinct to love is the instinct to desire and *to create*. The persistent tendency to de-sexualize, viewed as an *erasure* where sexual feelings or impulses are subtracted from an experience, has been described as a retreat from the threat of sexuality, hence a resultant desexualization. However, sexuality may also be *added* in order to transform some other threatening affect or impulse. In this way, sexuality can be used to defend against a variety of noxious feelings. *Sexualization as a defense* (Coen, 1992, 1998) is the repetitive and magical attempt to transform destructive feelings into excitement. These efforts usually depend on developmental issues and press. Sexualization can be used to transform vital urges, self-object deficits, preoedipal issues, grief, loss, competitiveness, envy, and/or hatred. In this vein, Kohut (1977) and Stolorow (1975) talked about *sexually expressed neediness*.

Sexualization can also be used to defend against itself, so to speak. Sexualization can transform other mental processes in order to displace erotic longing, as in so-called mental masturbation, the 'libidinization of thought' where thinking is disguised erotic gratification. The libidinization of reminiscence can be a defense against mourning and grief. The libidinization of perception (sexualized looking, voyeurism) can represent sexualization in order to hide sexual longing itself. "Sexual feelings seem so effectively to transform one's perceptions and feelings from bad to good" (Coen, 1992). The Marquis de Sade (1785) recommends sexualization for dealing with pain, "Nothing's villainous if it causes an erection" (p. 532). De Sade's motive: "One has got to learn to make the best of horror. There is in horror matter to produce an erection" and thereby it is possible to focus attention on this aspect in order to distract and transform horror to pleasure. All of these serve to express erotic longing in a safer arena thereby hiding vulnerability and threat. Incest is the acting on sexual urges in order to defend against separation, the resolution of oedipal conflict, and the denial of the difference between the generations (Chasseguet-Smirgel, 1999).

In general, sexualization as a defense precludes integration. It is a distraction, central to the so-called hysterical bargain (Myerson, 1969) and an inhibition of developmental progression. Sexualization is prominently involved in perversion, sadomasochistic relations, and pathological dependency. These can be used in any developmental constellation where there is an attempt to transform something noxious, intolerable, or otherwise distasteful into something wonderful and exciting.

Other erotic transferences are essentially *maternal erotic transferences* where nonverbal, body-based urges are expressed. These may include the desire for skin contact, merger wishes, the desire to suck, lick, and/or envelope the other – these are another version of erotic desire and are not genital but draw on the full range of erogenous zones in the body. The variety of erotic transferences centered on *oedipal dynamics* of competition and the desire to possess are well known. Finally, Bolognini (1994) introduced a healthier form of erotic transferences by delineating genuine, non-neurotic loving aspects of attachment, a so-called *affectionate transference* often emergent at the conclusion of an analysis.

Themes in erotic transferences

The classical model of erotic transferences was *oedipal*, those themes that revolve around *competition, envy, rivalry, and hierarchy*. This model did not take into account *maternal eroticism*, the sensual bonding between mother and baby. Contemporary models view these early determinants of erotic transferences as erotic in their own right. These are then rekindled in later genital sexuality. Early developmental stages are interwoven with the emergence of erotic transferences, such as the challenges of *sameness and difference* and, in an overall way, the *challenge of otherness*.

The mature capacity for love is an intersubjective and mutual achievement. This requires a sense of *separateness*, articulated selfhood, and capacities to be *intimate* (bodily close and mentally known) without fears of loss of self, such as are stimulated by unconscious fantasies of persecution, being overtaken, and/or annihilated. This line of development might be described as one from de-animation to becoming a subject of desire.

In this effort, we should resist the temptation to understand development in linear terms (as in psychosexual stages). The assumption underlying linear models is that once certain needs and phases are met, they are transcended and the individual then moves on to the next stage, such as in preoedipal lines to oedipal; oral to anal to genital, etc. Rather, these are recursive, ever-present dimensions of psychosexual experience and are better conceived as an ongoing dialectic.

Relationality/individuation is one such dialectic. It is through relational experience that we manifest our individuation (recognition and separation). It is through individuation that we can experience and survive intimacy (being seen and known). The danger inherent in the threat of intimacy for some is annihilation or fragmentation (while for others, the threat may revolve around castration, shame, or humiliation). These former threats reside at the level of identity and bodily integrity. *Intimacy and solitude* are in dialectical relation and not based on linear developmental theory. For one, this is an ongoing requirement of negotiation between sameness and difference.

In another domain, when working with erotic transferences, one cannot help but notice how interwoven are *sexuality and gender* development. It is helpful to have in mind the bisexual (and multi-sexual) nature of potentials in development as foundational to sexual development. Unlike anatomical sex, gender is a construction that may serve many purposes and ultimately resides fluidly in the psyche as a multiplicity. This opens up one's awareness of sexual and gender-related themes at every stage, especially as individuals become caught in various *binary traps*. Here, it is important to hold the possible resolution of these without pathologization.

One's sexuality goes beyond the anatomical to the very nature of our beings.[1] To encounter another person is to experience their being, to perceive their way of relating to others and the world. This includes their sexual being and the nature of their desires. It is to engage their humanity in their own particularized manner and style. When we 'see' another person, we immediately perceive their way of thinking, their relationship to their body, and their relationship to their sexuality, intelligence, strengths, gender, and desires.

In these ways, several categories of being are immediately present, especially one's sexuality and this is always inextricably intertwined with one's gender. It is through the expression of one's gender that we often perceive an individual's relationship to her or his sexuality, including but not limited to their sexual orientation, despite that we can often be mistaken about this.

Even when a person's gender is ambiguous, this is registered as such. All of these ways of experiencing ourselves in relation to others are captured in the essential fact of how we enter into the world, always embodied, always sentient, sexed, and gendered. It is helpful to emphasize the distinction between the way in which our anatomical bodies are sexed as opposed to the ways in which we develop our gendered identities, in other words, the sense and style, experience, and expression of being a man or woman (masculinity and femininity, in whatever way these are understood and expressed).

In an overall way, and from within the position of the experiencing self (the experiencer/agent or embodied subject), individual experience can be described as some amalgam of *receptivity and potency* – in the language of sexuality, *holding and penetration* or, in the language of the body, *openness and backbone*. Put as a more traditional stereotype: the feminine and masculine,[2] but here representing bi-gendered aspects of the self as opposed to one over the other. Indeed, to describe phenomenal experience from the position of the *embodied subject*, I am describing this dialectic, the experiencer/agent as a position where one has achieved some blend of *access to feeling* (*receptivity*) and *articulated selfhood* (*potency*).

Gender is one of many difference markers (Goldner, 1991) that poses a binary facilitating the organization of an early self, as the preoedipal child awakens to sex and gender differences. In Goldner's (1991) words, "Gender [is] a transcendent social category whose truth, though false, remains central to thought" (p. 70). Other binaries may serve the same purpose (see, for example, Stoller [1968] and Chodorow [2011] for a discussion of the way gender may be used as an organizer of separation, Chodorow [2011] for a discussion of the little girl/mother polarity, Chasseguet-Smirgel [1984] for a discussion of generational difference, and Laplanche [1997] for a discussion of the child's negotiation of the primal scene). These sexed and gendered splits often form the basis of segregated or dissociated aspects of the self that need to be recuperated and reconnected, as in the post-oedipal recuperation of earlier bi-sexual self-other identifications (Bassin, 1996; Benjamin, 1998; Elise, 2002; See Celenza, 2012 for a discussion of how gendered splits can collude in the organization of cross-gendered identifications).

My stance is to engage this polarity (receptivity and potency), stereotypically definitional of femininity and masculinity, in order to expose this polarity as a false dichotomy, the poles of which are not actually opposite (thereby are not mutually exclusive) in any register of meaning. These reckonings and the particular individual's negotiation of each may define the ways in which sex and gender are instantiated, experienced, and expressed from within the embodied subject. They may also vary *intra*-individually as relational patterns shift and self-experience multiplies and expands. *Most importantly, I view these poles as liberated from any hierarchic power relation, in that neither pole is privileged*, though in any particular individual one may be.[3] Even in its disavowal, each pole of this duality will be relevant, along with multiple gendered and nongendered dualities revolving around this "force field" (Dimen, 1991). This is what I mean to convey with the play on Faulkner's (1951) phrase, *The binary is not dead; it is not even binary.*

One aim of clinical practice is to liberate our patients from constraint and degradation in the construction of self-referents, of which gender is a foundational organizer. An aspect of the initial engagement in the clinical setting involves the adoption (temporarily) of our patients' language (gender stereotypes being "available as consensual linguistic categories" [Stein, 1995b, p. 308]) in order to join each individual in her or his way of organizing subjective experience and their relation to the world. As treatment progresses, it becomes possible to transcend cultural stereotypes (of gender, race, ethnicity, age, etc.) and expand self-experience and gender repertoire (Elise, 1998, 2019; see Stein, 1995a for an elaboration of clinical process with a transsexual patient; see Long, 2005 for a panel report on the function of binary systems in promoting cross-classification). This expansion involves the acceptance and inclusion of binarial, oppositional categories in a both/and multiplicity, in effect to achieve a *unique gender blend*.[4] This blend reveals the gender binary as a false dichotomy and guards against polarization in favor of a playful oscillation between the two and the many (see Harris, 2005 and Goldner, 1991 for extensive development of this idea).

Through the language of multiplicity and binarial transcendence, I aim to advance the idea that gender identity is not only fluid, but ultimately internal. The sense of receptivity (a capacity to take in) along with the capacity to stand firm, put out (so to speak) are both foundational to strength and health. Ultimately, neither are sexed or gendered and at the same time both are essential (not in an anatomical sense, but in the sense of the attainment of healthy, human capacities which may form the goals (among others) of psychoanalysis.

Signifiers of the erotic, identifications, introjects, and signifiers of the abject

Prior to the developmental challenge of transcending binaries, however, is the pre-binarial condition of infancy, before the baby is aware of anatomical sex difference and when its relationship to its body can be thought of as *pre-gendered*. Lombardi (2016) speaks of a vertical axis wherein the first condition of life is somatosensory, a corporeal condition where concrete somatic sensations precede introjective processes. This domain revolves around the subjective experience of being a body and the infant's relation to it. In the horizontal axis, the primary caregiver ministers to the baby and aids in the experience of safely dwelling within one's own body. From an intersubjective perspective, I will be developing the idea of *the first signifier*[5] *of the erotic* as a *body-based feminine.* This is derived from the infant's experience of its body *as held, soothed, and stimulated by the maternal*[6] *figure*, i.e., the experience of the mother with her infant. This includes, of course, the breast, and raises the theoretical problem that this breast is generally discussed as *a de-eroticized breast*, good or bad, but not erotic.[7] Yet, it remains that through body-based ministrations and the primary caregiver's empathic recognition and love, the maternal figure initiates and for a time, comprises the baby's entire relation to the world. The primary caregiver comes to represent, thereby, the first signifier of the infant's vitalized relation to its body.

In a more specific way and through a nonsexed, nongendered lens, (women do not own the feminine [Kristeva, 2019]), the primal and originary experience with a primary caregiver develops the first signifier of the erotic. This experience comes to represent what we call the *feminine*, (to speak of one pole of the traditional gender binary) through the breast or nipple-bottle-breast.[8] Most importantly, this occurs within the relationship between the primary caregiver and infant, because it is when the infant is receptively helpless to the ministrations of the primary object, when our *taking in* of the world is wholly dependent on the satisfying and frustrating primary caregiver, i.e., the good and bad signifier of the nipple-bottle-breast.

If women no longer own the feminine, then what I mean to convey is the way in which the infant experiences the primary caregiver's ministrations, probing and receptive to the infant's needs. These come to represent the signifiers of the nipple-bottle-breast, the first signifiers of the body-based feminine.[9]

Though not a theoretically settled issue (see Birksted-Breen, 1996), many psychoanalytic authors believe that ideas about a *core* or *primary* femininity (especially as these ideas are linked to anatomical metaphors) have been superseded in favor of a psychic bi- or multi-sexuality (see, for example, Harris [2005], Celenza [2014] and Perelberg [2018]). Whether or not one accepts the idea of a primary femininity, the tendency to split representations of the feminine (or to polarize the feminine and masculine) continues to be found in analytic work. Splitting or polarization is the first step in a defensive process of the many forms of disavowal, the next step being degradation of the disavowed side. For example, intense longings for closeness or dependency can be held in mind as 'feminine' *and thereby weak*. Problems with assertiveness can likewise be associated with 'feminine' submissiveness, and thus devalued. Such significations serve to defensively split psychic capacities, relegating certain personality characteristics to disavowed, dissociated, unrepresented, or repressed self-states.[10]

Internalization processes, especially as a response to absence or loss, comprise the ways in which the psyche constitutes itself, i.e., the structures of subjectivity. These structures differ to varying degrees, especially in the extent to which they are more or less ego-syntonic versus those that are repressed, disavowed, or otherwise foreclosed.[11] *Identification* represents the harmonious form of internalization in contrast to incorporation and introjection (Schafer, 1968; Laplanche and Pontalis, 1973; Akhtar, 2009). Indeed, we can say that one way in which processes of internalization are distinguished relates to the degree of harmony and ego-syntonicity that define and differentiate them.

To be specific, the psychoanalytic definition of identification is

Psychological process whereby the subject assimilates an aspect, property or attribute of the other and is transformed, wholly or partially, after the model the other provides. It is by means of a series of identifications that the personality is constituted and specified.

(Laplanche and Pontalis, 1973, p. 205)

Through this definition and the distinctions among internalization processes, it is possible to see that identification as the central unconscious process for coping with loss (and for the constitution of identity) does not require a repudiation of the characteristics thereby assimilated. Rather, a repudiated signifier is, by definition, not an identification but an introject. Here, foreclosure, eradication, repression, and/or degradation are implicated in internalizing processes (as in incorporation and introjection).

In contrast to identification, *introjection* (and its end-product, introject) is defined by:

The organized cluster of memory traces ... remain[ing] unassimilated in the total self image ...Identifications, unlike introjects, do not feel like a 'foreign body' in the self and are more likely to be ego-syntonic and in harmony with the individual's self-image.

(Akhtar, 2009, p. 150)

It is reasonable to conclude that *repudiated or abject* (in this case, gendered) *signifiers* are internalized as pathological *introjects*, a site of conflict, dystonicity, and disavowal where the individual is in some measure at war with herself. The analyst, in contrast, offers an opportunity for identification through identificatory love (albeit, a love that is not to be had in a sexual sense) without repudiation in the sense of condemnation or degradation. Due to the analyst's ability to contain the projected attacks, these internalizations become usable modes of being that transform the inner psychic presences to a more benign presence.

Disavowed 'things' that are sensed as foreign, unwanted, or 'not me' fragments (including those outside of the signified), are, by definition, not identifications but introjects. Here, foreclosure, eradication, repression, repudiation, and/or dissociation are implicated in internalization processes. It is reasonable to conjecture that disavowed or otherwise unwanted signifiers can be internalized as pathological introjects. Signifiers of the abject are one type of introject and, by virtue of representing a part of the mother's body, *introjected part-objects*.

Through a totalistic conception of erotic desire, it can be more usefully stated that the *repudiation* of femininity in the move from dyadic to triadic relations is unnecessary, especially repudiation in the sense of *rejection with disapproval and/or condemnation*. In addition, repudiation need not be linked to associations of femininity as passivity, submission, or other aspects of a devalued, alien self, eventuating in the splitting of the ego-ideal, especially for girls.

It is necessary to resist this divisive impulse, enlarging the analyst's capacity to experience our patients and the analytic process with the full range of affectivity at our disposal. The recognition of a multi-gendered and multi-sexuality within ourselves will resonate and nurture these identifications within our patients. This is facilitated by transcending the false binarial constructions of femininity and masculinity as well as the feminine ideal and repudiated signifiers of the feminine.

Maternal eroticism in the analytic situation

Many components of Kristeva's[12] understanding of maternal eroticism coincide with the offerings of the analytic situation, a fundamental provocation for maternal transferences. There are positive features that contribute to the safety of the setting, offering our patients experiences toward (re)-vitalization, "a listener, a receiver, as much as for an object" (Widawsky, 2014, p. 65). Winnicott's (1960) expression of the holding environment is included here as is Laplanche's (1999) more general reference to the analyst's binding work derived from the life instinct. In line with this theorizing, (but without direct reference to the erotic *per se*) is Winnicott's (1960, 1971) 'potential space' referring to the good-enough mother's facilitation of the child's capacity to think and create. Green (1986) refers to the analyst's provision of a framing structure, much like the mother's holding the child in her arms. Bion's (1970) negative capability might be viewed as the mental level of this framing structure, providing an affirmative space for whatever the patient brings.

There are *inherent, implicit* manifestations of the erotic dimensions in the analytic situation. Metaphorically, it can be said that the treatment situation encompasses both containing and penetrating functions of the analyst, a *taking in* and *penetrating into* interplay (Celenza, 2014) that can capture the ways in which the erotic is conveyed in a mutual regulatory fashion. The erotic carries within it a vitalization in *receiving* stimuli and *fueling* forces, both of which invest in life. As noted in the previous chapter, analytic process can be experienced as both penetrating and enveloping, incisive and holding, a firm receptivity that retains, envelops, and holds the other in mind (Celenza, 2014). These metaphors reflect the ways in which analytic process does its re-vitalizing work.

Further, erotic transferences manifest the analysand's vitality, in its most intense, sometimes sexual form. While in the past, erotic transferences have been perceived as resistances to the treatment (and certainly can function defensively), contemporary theorizing views the emergence of erotic transferences as natural, healthy, and promoting of the analysand's creativity while its avoidance, a defensive resistance (Celenza, 2014, 2022a; Davies, 1998a, b; Elise, 2019). *We could say that erotic transferences (and erotic countertransferences) are the vehicles for the revitalizing work of the analytic process.*

Notes

1 See Celenza (2014) for a more elaborated discussion of these themes.
2 I realize articulating this binary can be misunderstood as promoting one pole over the other, in line with the ways in which Western culture traditionally organizes sexual and gendered splits. I am not supporting the traditional delegation of a host of (gendered and nongendered) relations associated with each pole to either female or male (e.g., femininity with passivity, to name the most prevalent). Risking this misunderstanding, I am proposing the articulation of this binary because it is helpful in describing clinical problems, ways in which individuals are trapped in gender polarities and splits, *with the clinical aim of transcending these* (see Dimen [1991] and Benjamin [1998] for further discussion of splitting and its interface with gender polarity).

3 Compare Schiller's (2012) framework of female sexuality that she conceives as 'existing alongside' the traditional phallocentric framework.

4 Along similar lines, Lingiardi (2007) discusses the ways in which refusing forced binaries does not mean defending the gray area equidistant from the two extremes.

5 I have selected the term *signifier* to connote *carrier of (conscious or unconscious) meaning*. I do not use the term in the context of Lacanian theorizing, but prefer the term *signifier* to symbol, imago, representation, and various types of internalization because signifier is general in its connotation and does not specify a form (i.e. verbal, nonverbal, unrepresented) or mode of internalization.

6 I use the term *maternal* and *feminine* to describe the primary caregiver, whom we know is not necessarily a woman.

7 One exception is Hilferding (1911/1974) who wrote about the erogenous breast.

8 I use the phrase nipple-bottle-breast in order to depict maternal ministrations, inclusive of mothers who are not women.

9 In a similar vein, the Oedipal complex has to be reformulated through a nongendered lens, conveying the crucial developmental challenge for the toddler to cope with the move from dyadic to triangular relations – better referred to as the move from two to three than from female to male.

10 See Essay 20, *From foreclosed void to usable space* (Celenza, 2022a) for a clinical application of these ideas.

11 See, for example, Butler (1995) for a description of the daughter's incorporative identification as a disavowed homosexual attachment to the mother. (I disagree, however, with Butler's use of the term identification in this context.)

12 Kristeva's (2014a,b) theorizing of maternal eroticism is discussed in detail in Chapter 5.

Chapter 3

Maternal *erotic* transferences

In 1931, Freud beckoned female analysts to gain access to preoedipal transferences in analyses with female patients. Over the past century, we have seen many clinical reports from female analysts involving theorizing in the preoedipal domain. Until recent decades, *erotic* transferences (presumably, oedipal) seemed to remain the purview of male analysts. Clinical lore held the mistaken idea that female analysts did not (perhaps could not) evoke erotic transferences and it was surmised that, at least with male patients, this was related to the intolerable helplessness associated with dependency longings in the maternal transference (Chasseguet-Smirgel, 1976; Lester, 1985; Person, 1985; Kernberg, 1994). Female analysts (and male analysts as well) can collude with this clinical lore by taking refuge in a *de-eroticized* maternal transference and countertransference. There may be several reasons for this defensive move, including discomfort with erotic material in the transference/countertransference interplay (Coen, 1994; Gabbard, 1994a; Davies, 1998b; Celenza, 2014, 2022a, b; Elise, 2019) and/or various kinds of discomfort in combining the maternal[1] with the erotic.

As noted in the Introduction, such de-erotization and specifically de*sexualization* have been identified in psychoanalytic theorizing of the maternal. For example, Balsam (2012, 2019) addresses the neglect of the female body in psychoanalytic literature and Litowitz (2014) wonders if the mother's body has been *denatured* in object relations theories. In recent decades, the recognition of the maternal transference *as erotic* is emerging in the literature (see, for examples, Chasseguet-Smirgel, 1970, 1976; McDougall, 1986, 1995; Kulish, 1989; Wrye and Welles, 1994; Benjamin, 1995; Elise, 2002, 2015, 2017, 2019; Dimen, 2003; Harris, 2005; Fonagy and Target, 2007; Balsam, 2012, 2014, 2019;

DOI: 10.4324/9781003391012-3

Salomonsson, 2012; Kristeva, 2000, 2011, 2014a, b; Litowitz, 2014; Widawsky, 2014; Wilson, 2014; Celenza, 2014, 2022a, b; Atlas, 2016). These authors and discussions have marked an important shift in analytic theorizing.

Identificatory love

Early forms of erotic transferences can involve desires to deny separateness and fantasies of merger. Such erotic transferences are not gender-specific and can emerge regardless of the sexual orientation of either analyst or analysand. These types of transferences refer to early developmental stages of longing, and are pre-symbolic and sensual. These desires predate the consolidation of subjectivity and are particularly threatening due to the experiences of annihilation and/or loss of self as the desire for the other is aroused. This type of longing is referred to as identificatory love because of the experience of loss of identity, i.e., the desire *to be* (versus object love which refers to the desire *to have*).

Freud, in his heteronormative construction of the Oedipus complex, splits identificatory love and object love in his attempt to account for gender identification and sexual orientation – unfortunately degrading the 'negative' oedipal position along the way. Later theorizing elaborated various mechanisms of internalization, including those from a developmental perspective. These retained the idea of separate mechanisms at different points on the developmental ladder. Gaddini (1969), for example, distinguished between early imitations (associated with omnipotent fantasies in line with the pleasure principle) and early identifications (or introjections, more in line with the reality principle) as the young child struggles with becoming (*to be*) versus desiring (*to have*).

All of these internalization processes address frustrations with separation and loss. Many other theorists had earlier written about these distinctions in various ways (cf. Ferenczi, 1932a, b; Fenichel, 1937; Deutsch, 1942; Eidelberg, 1948; Federn, 1952; Ritvo and Provence, 1953; Greenacre, 1958; Greenson, 1966; Stoller, 1966). Though many of these writers aim to distinguish among internalization processes, later developmental stages are characterized by a blending of imitation, introjection, and identification as the distinction between being and having seems to fall away in later years.

Perhaps in a move toward a totalistic view of erotic and sexual love, Freud himself later theorized the relationship between identification and object love in a more combinatory way, establishing identification as an initial stage of object choice.

> Preliminary stages of love emerge … [in] the first of these aims, we recognize the phase of incorporating or devouring – a type of love which is consistent with abolishing the object's separate existence.
>
> (1915b, p. 138)

And then again, in a later paper,

> [I]dentification is a *preliminary stage* of object-choice, that it is the first way – and one that is expressed in an ambivalent fashion – in which the ego picks out an object. The ego wants to incorporate this object into itself, and, in accordance with the oral or cannibalistic phase of libidinal development in which it is, it was to do so by devouring it.
>
> (Freud, 1917, pp. 249–250, *italics added*)

In these excerpts, it appears Freud was attempting to contend with the threat associated with object choice (and the ego's attempt to omnipotently control the object of desire by devouring it).

Developmental contexts

Maternal erotic transferences are comprised of the sensual bonding between mother and baby. Contemporary models view early determinants of erotic transferences as erotic in their own right. These are then rekindled in later genital sexuality. Wrye and Welles (1994) speak of "body loveprinting" (p. 34) derived from maternal ministrations with bodily experience, including skin contact and contact with all manner of bodily fluids as juicy, gooey, and messy. When I nurtured my infant sons, I would often say, "Nothing is eew that comes out of you." The fantasies of maternal infant bonding comprise powerful sensory imagery of nursing, putting together, getting inside, pouring, patting, poking, smearing, and messing (Wrye and Welles, 1994, p. 36). This can be indicated in the countertransference by a stirring counterpart. I treated a man who had a childhood history of severe maternal neglect.

Never had I had such a strong desire to touch a patient, to stroke his hair, to touch his skin in some reassuring and loving gesture.

Wrye and Welles (1994) describe four interrelated narratives manifest in maternal erotic transferences. The first is comprised of body-based aspects of self and signal the birth of desire. It is here that active seeking of sensual reciprocity occurs through feeding, bathing, cooing, and holding. The analysand expresses longing for an erotic sensual relationship in concrete, nonverbal forms. "These bodily sensations are not symbolic of sexual contact; they *are* the contact … bodily feelings are the stuff of these archaic transferences" (p. 58). This quest attempts to re-create the earliest experience of the transformational environmental mother, who is less an object than a process, who is able to, through her bodily ministrations to the infant, 'alter self experience' (Bollas, 1987, p. 58 fn).

The second stage is characterized by anal erotism and permutations of desire. These include positive and negative fantasy recreations of anal themes, e.g., containment, expulsion, spoiling, valuation, and anal birth. Sadomasochistic and obsessive-compulsive symptomatology are characteristic of this stage.

The sensual matrix of object relations characterizes the third stage. This includes part- to whole-object relations, therapist fantasied as container, attempts at integration, and ambivalence. Finally, there is the solidification of gender identity. This usually oscillates between preoedipal and oedipal phenomena as the individual attempts to consolidate gender identity.

Chasseguet-Smirgel (1970) adds to these conceptualizations by describing female sexuality. She includes male fantasies about terrifying females and women's guilty fantasies about their instinctual impulses, termed feminine guilt. At the time of change of oedipal object, a kind of splitting occurs where the bad object is associated with the mother and the good object is projected onto the father. When reality does not correct this problem (i.e., when mothers are actually castrating or sadistic and fathers are benign and loving) severe problems can occur. For example, oedipal positions can become a haven and psychical refuge that require a contrasting dangerous externality in the real world.

McDougall (1992) describes the baby's earliest reality as her/his mother's unconscious in the form of primitive communication and "neo-needs" (p. 274). Karen Horney (1933) wrote about the denial of the vagina. She tried to answer the question of why vaginal excitations become repressed, centering around castration wishes and fears toward the father, linked with Oedipal frustrations and wishes for revenge. Her stance was that 'the undiscovered vagina is a vagina denied' or, in other words, a defense. For girls, the fear of castration is complicated because she cannot reassure herself that her fears are unfounded. This is further complicated because the vagina is invisible. The girl fears above all, injuries inside her body. She represses her vaginal impulses and transfers them to her external organ, the clitoris, for purposes of defense. Though many of these ideas are now supplanted by contemporary views, the history of our literature can be helpful in understanding certain inhibitions or outmoded but consequential conscious or unconscious convictions in our patients.

Benjamin (1995) theorizes that an erotic transference is the idealization of the analyst as the bestower of recognition, i.e., the one who knows, or could know, the patient. To be known or recognized is immediately to experience the other's power. This may evoke awe, dread, admiration, or adoration as well as humiliation or exhilarating submission (p. 149). This is a different metaphor for the maternal form of knowledge as power, thereby casting a different slant on the Angel, the ideal, and the love of knowledge as power (i.e., in contrast to the phallocentric view).

Benjamin goes on,

> Further contesting the paternal-phallic idea of the analyst who is idealized as the "one supposed to know" is the idea of the analyst as "the one who knows *me*." This contrast coincides with the typical gender pairings: masculine/universal versus feminine/particular, masculine/abstract versus feminine/personal. The one who empathically understands, who is emotionally attuned to me, is associated with maternal functions of holding, containing and attuning. This knowing, like the paternal erotic, is also subject to idealization and evokes longings for unattainable fulfillment.
>
> (Benjamin, 1995, p. 159)

This maternal imagery, on theoretical grounds, becomes associated with holding and containing as well as the creation of space, preverbal dialogue associated with mother-infant interaction and other pre-symbolic forms of interaction schemas. These are contrasted with the penetrative, insight-oriented forms of being associated with phallic, paternal imagery.

Chetrit-Vatine (2004) derives her theorizing from Levinas (1961) and Laplanche (1997, 1999) by emphasizing the ethical seduction that occurs between analyst and patient, mirroring the primal seduction of the maternal figure. Parsing the receptivity of the primary caregiver, she notes Levinas' description of the caress, the face, and the saying. Here, the caress addresses the other by accessing the other through the maternal gaze, the face, or as I suggest, "le visage de la mère" (Celenza, 2022a).

All of these writers are, from different angles and emphases, attempting to describe facets of the maternal containing transference (Modell, 1990), "matricial space" (Chetrit-Vatine, 2004), or the 'emergent/ reliance of maternal eroticism' (Kristeva, 2014a), i.e., ways in which the recognition of otherness bestow and constitute the rudiments of subjectivity.

JULIA: Longing for sameness and merger wishes

"I'm happy for her, she's always wanted to be married. But I don't want that for myself." Julia, a single woman painter and dancer, will now be living alone as her roommate moves out of their apartment to live with her fiancé. Suddenly, I'm aware of my wedding band on this, our first session, and I feel Julia's gaze weighing heavily on my finger. "I want a steady boyfriend but haven't been able to find one. It upsets me, but mostly, I'm worried about my career. I hate the spotlight and don't like to show my work. I just give my paintings away."

Despite these initial complaints, Julia's appeal to me was a feeling of her basic sense of optimism which I saw as poignant and charming yet also naïve. She spoke of her childhood as uneventful and happy, recounting stories in a blasé way that to me held potentially traumatic aspects. She told me of her birth, "I was planned. My parents were hoping for a boy." Perhaps in a deft move of exacting revenge in the present, she then described her mother's experience in labor (long and painful).

At the start of analysis, Julia did not identify her sexuality as a problem area despite that she came to analysis for problems with intimacy. She saw her difficulty with intimacy as separate from her sexuality, preferring to view herself as sexually unconventional and uninhibited. She told me that in the past, she had enjoyed sexual experiences that involved multiple partners and, at times, recreational drugs (specifically, marijuana and ecstasy). She did not view either as problematic yet worried that I might see it that way. She grew up with many siblings in a fairly chaotic home atmosphere; I wondered what she was recreating through her sexuality and drug use.

Julia's first sexual experience as a teenager was (in her mind at the time) consciously designed to experiment with her body and break down inhibitions. This experience involved seducing three men sequentially on the same day (privately, in different locations and none knew of the others). In her young adulthood, she continued to experiment sexually, but often in a distanced, sometimes drug-induced state. Jealousies and competitive feelings conflicted with her desires to be uninhibited and sexually carefree, so she gradually became monogamous, however she then experienced difficulty sustaining a relationship, where either she or the man would lose interest.[2]

"I usually want things men don't. I want a *merger*," Julia told me one day. She described this longing – her word was merger – as a quasi-hypnotic experience of being totally understood, known, and cared for without having to say or do anything herself. Months later, she would tell me how frustrated she was that I could not automatically know her mind. She felt frustrated at the effort it took to speak her thoughts and feelings. She expressed a desire for me to know her through some kind of body therapy, touch therapy, or some way to magically bypass having to speak. She expressed wishes that I could read her mind, get inside her skin, and know her without her having to say anything.

Julia continued to complain that talking was too intellectual and "left-brain." During this time, she frequently sought out therapies that were more body-oriented, involving massage and reading "auras" around her body. I said, "It's wonderful to be touched without words, to be understood effortlessly, totally." She said words divided us and that they did not describe how she wanted to be transformed. She wanted to *feel* different and she wanted me to *make her feel* different without her having to say anything, by touching her body, or in some spiritual, ineffable way. She said she didn't care about knowing – *why*, *how*, or even *what* she wanted – she just wanted me to *do* it. I felt the intensity of her frustrations and wishes; there was urgency. I acknowledged her wish that I change her and how powerful that would make me. (I felt her wish for my power yet at the same time, I felt powerless and constrained. Just what was it she wanted me to *do*?) She said she felt exhausted with being the powerful one and wanted me to take over. She wanted to say nothing and do nothing herself.

At the same time, Julia expressed the feeling that I was hurting her with insights, 'doing to her' by making *observations of* her that may have held some truth on an intellectual level but did not change how she felt in her real life. I suggested that words made her feel I was outside of her, *not in it with her* so that she felt alone in my presence. She said this was similar to her experience of her father, an intellectual researcher who would regularly conduct experiments in the kitchen (i.e., in the family eating and living space). She felt this was a way he ignored the family's basic needs and displayed his self-centeredness. Maleness came to be defined to Julia as intrusive, self-absorbed, intellectually aggressive, and disconnected. I felt as if I could hurt her with my 'male' tools of analysis and insights that were different from her (i.e., outside her perspective). In contrast, she wanted a 'female' kind of loving from me, one where I shared her perspective completely, non-intellectually, and nonverbally. To Julia, sameness was maternal and healing whereas paternality conjured difference and harm.

Soon it became clear that among the reasons for Julia's objections to analysis was a deep sadness that she could not *be inside my womb.*[3] Together, we recognized the sensual aspects of her desires, her wish that she was my baby, that I might give her my breast, she feeding on my body, that she could *be inside my body* and I inside her, to touch her, and feel her being from the inside. I became increasingly sensitized to her need for me to express my recognition of her internal states, especially painful experiences such as the birth of her siblings and other experiences that reflected early deprivations. I became more expressive to her of these needs and linked them to her mother's passivity and seeming lack of interest in her. I appreciated the erotic nature of these longings in her as well, i.e., longings to be touched, stimulated, or sensually aroused by my body, to be lost in the feelings of it and her desires to have me long for her in the same ways.

As the analysis proceeded, Julia began to wonder if she wanted to be with a man at all. She expressed the desire to be loved by a man who was more like a woman. She understood her desire (for a womanly man) as expressing a frustration in the way men are socialized in our culture and not as a homosexual longing because she was not aware of being stimulated by or erotically fantasizing about me or other women. She had many close women friends and had experimented sexually with one, but stated that she did not fantasize about women erotically, the way she fantasized about men. She realized that what she longed for was "not a man, I want a mouth."

I felt Julia was expressing both male and female modes of relating (as she had come to define these). First (and by now a familiar pattern) was the desire to be merged with me as a denial of our separateness; Julia associated these desires with a maternal or female mode of relating, us being inside each other, *a taking in*. She told childhood stories of being left alone, a constant feeling of not being loved or cared for by her mother who she increasingly recognized as chronically depressed. In contrast (and with much complaint and discomfort for Julia) was the persistently frustrating, insight-oriented mode of relating where she felt pressured *to speak* and *to know* the meaning of her desires. Julia associated this form of relating with maleness, a kind of intellectual and disconnected, intrusive, and penetrating form of engagement, a *doing to*.

Paradoxically, I reminded Julia that 'being done to' was something she had persistently demanded of me – she wanted me to *do something to* her without her having to do anything in return. Receptivity took on more complexity: she realized being receptive to my attunement meant allowing penetration of *both my sameness and difference*. She began to notice that indeed she wanted both: attunement and penetration, sameness and difference, me inside her, and she inside me. (This eventually led to an expansion of her self-experience and a manner of her phenomenal experiencing beyond a simple male/female or masculine/feminine binary.)

In the last year of analysis, Julia wondered if I shared similar conflicts and how I might manage them with my husband. She said,

> Well, I know you're a professional and you stand for things. But we're in such different worlds. I don't want what you want. I don't want kids, living in the suburbs, a house, and conventional-type things. Your husband is probably Caucasian. I am turned on by ethnic types. Diversity is very important to me.

She noted a tendency to become involved with "exotic-looking" men who she then experienced as masculine but narcissistic, "in their own world." Alternatively, she experienced "WASP-y" men as passive and effeminate, with whom she became frustrated and then experienced as weak. (These are all her characterizations.) She felt confused about desiring too much, of being too hungry; she struggled with being attracted to men who couldn't return her interest or who didn't seem to want enough and couldn't match the intensity of her passion.

She began to question how to resolve being a strong woman without fearing overpowering a man.

At this time, Julia became more curious about my 'insides,' asking questions about what I feel toward men, how I express my needs sexually, and whether I am satisfied. I heard these questions on two levels: both as a question about her feminine sexuality (i.e., what was inside her and whether any man could satisfy her needs) and as an expression of how she fantasized we were negotiating our needs together. While in the past, the question was, Were we one person or two? Now the question was gendered: were we two women or a man and a woman? Who would be on top? She previously had longed to merge with me in a nongendered way, as person to person. Now, not only was her experience with me gendered, Julia seemed interested in me *as a man.* What was inside me? Was I big and powerful? How does a man satisfy me? On an unconscious level, was there a man inside me that she could access?

Julia began to show her work publically. She sold many paintings and won awards. She began to feel 'big' inside herself.[4] As these changes took place in her outside life, she also began to experience herself as a strong woman, a 'manly' woman yet feminine at the same time. It is possible to play with these emerging self-states in a gendered way: the man inside the woman, the womanly man, the mother and the little boy inside, the little girl – all of them reflecting a partial truth and none comprising, by itself, the whole. As the analysis drew to a close, it was evident that Julia had increasing access to a fuller range.

MICHAEL: To be or to have?

Whether or not a patient arouses sexual desire in the analyst is an important indicator of the patient's vitality and strength, their sense of wholeness or coherence. What if there is *no* sexual desire in relation to the patient? This should not be confused with the analyst's subjective experience of neutrality or an easy route to abstinence. The absence of erotic energy (mutual and bi-directional) should prompt the analyst to explore inhibitions or other conflicts. In this way, it might be viewed as a *present absence.*

I've written extensively about Michael whose erotic imaginings toward me became the central focus early on in his treatment (Celenza, 2006a, 2010, 2014). An inhibited, obsessional academic who had grown up with divorced parents, largely in the care of his domineering, narcissistic mother, Michael became preoccupied with the wish to have sex with me after about a year into the treatment.

Michael is a 45-year-old Mathematics professor who was in analysis with me for six years. His concerns initially revolved around long-standing problems with impotence and difficulty accessing his desires in general. He had always been successful at work but had difficulty sustaining romantic relationships. Historically, he had become involved with women he desired but quickly felt dominated by, prompting the ending of the relationship, usually by her. He inevitably felt demeaned and humiliated. He noticed that his relationships lasted longer if he did not fall in love. In his mid-30s, he married a female friend, sustaining a constricted, passionless relationship for about five years. They divorced having never consummated their marriage. Michael then retreated into relative isolation.

About the middle of the year 1999, Michael became increasingly preoccupied with the Y2K crisis and became convinced that civilization was about to end. He stockpiled food and water. It was around this time that he began treatment with me as his anxiety over Y2K mounted. Several months later and still a few months shy of the turn of the century, he bought a gun in the belief that he would need to defend his stockpiles from desperately starving people. He also began taking shooting lessons.

Michael became obsessed with the idea that the world was going to be caught unaware and that though there was talk of fixing the computer problem, in reality no one was helping. He was convinced there was going to be a panic. Desperately needy people were going to break into his house, kill him, and steal his supplies. He dug a trench in his backyard where he buried his canned food. He worried for my safety. I wondered if he were psychotic.

Throughout this early and intensely anxious period, we worked on establishing links from his current ruminations to his childhood experience. His mother was a 'desperately needy' woman who demanded high achievements but displayed no interest in his emotional wellbeing. She would burst into his room 'catching him unaware' and rant about some chore he hadn't finished. His father was of 'no help,' uninvolved, and living apart since his parents divorced. I noted too that it was he who was furious, wanting to kill people, but he denied this.

As Michael got older, he felt exploited and enslaved. As an example, his mother would have dinner parties where he would be required to greet the guests, hang up their coats, and serve dinner. He felt particularly demeaned when his mother insisted he wear a napkin over his arm, which he thought made the guests laugh at him. He took refuge in his schoolwork. He was a math prodigy so he set off for college at 16, relieved but psychologically unprepared.

Michael's anxiety began to settle down as we made the links from childhood to his Y2K construction. He said these links "made sense" and he began to feel less crazy. Several weeks before New Year's Eve, he turned his gun over to the police. Still, his obsessive anxieties about a Y2K catastrophe persisted (though diminished from "a 99% likelihood to a 20% likelihood," expressed in true mathematician style) and these anxieties had a real effect on me. As the final week of 1999 counted down, I did what any self-respecting psychoanalyst, deeply immersed in a psychoanalytic dyad, might do. I went to Costco and stockpiled six cases of Pellegrino.

When Y2K fantasies never materialized, Michael was embarrassed but also curious about how he could have gone to such extremes. This prompted his desire for psychoanalysis and though I wondered about his stability, I agreed.

During the first year of analysis, Michael revealed,

> I have a conflict. On the one hand, I feel you're a good analyst. You strive to help me. But it feels like love. And you will not reveal anything about your personal life. Like a blind man develops a heightened sense of hearing or touch, I read you. I want to praise you and tell you about all of your qualities. But you won't give anything back. How am I supposed to do this one-sided thing?

Here, Michael explicitly referred to the structured imbalance in the analytic dyad and the way he experienced the asymmetric distribution of attention. I thought he was telling me that this felt simultaneously stimulating, gratifying, and frustrating. Michael specifically articulated these factors over time and as his frustration grew, he developed a shorthand for his experience of 'the analytic set-up.' He became fond of rephrasing the Hippocratic Oath as my "Hypocritical Oath," referring to my refusal to engage in a sexual relationship with him as hypocritical, given the seductive and tempting aspects of the psychoanalytic situation.

Interestingly, I noticed that I was actually *less* revealing and more constrained with Michael than is typical of my style, despite the fact that he demanded more and seemed particularly pained by my reserve.

What was the nature of this aspect of my countertransference? I did not know yet, but the awareness of my relatively greater constraint with Michael increased my guilt.

I recognized the cautionary themes in the literature, especially the potential inhibitory effects of the female analyst's discomfort with power, so I stood my ground. I recognized an unmistakeable feeling that I was *doing something to* Michael, as if by virtue of being his analyst I was hurting him. He seemed to blame me for paying exclusive attention to him, for doing the very job he had hired me to do. In order to tolerate my guilt, I frequently reminded myself that his humiliation and difficulty accepting the treatment frame derived from his childhood experiences. He was not wrong in what he was saying, he was just stuck on it. I openly acknowledged the accuracy of his observations about the power imbalance between us, but I maintained my analytic stance and steeled myself for a fight.

Michael came to our next session telling me he was thinking about me entirely too much. He described aching, longing fantasies of making love with me, talking to me about his desires, and stated,

> I'm imagining you watching me. I have a fantasy about you. We have sex, it's mutual, ecstatic, loving. We each leave our partners and live together forever. I want that. But I worry I may not be able to keep up with you. You have so many interests. And sexually too.

Noting the allusion to his performance anxiety, I said, "You worry you won't be able to keep up?" He responded, "I do tend to feed off the other person's life. I'd get involved in what you like. I'd be interested – I'd be your surrogate."

In this interchange Michael revealed a merger fantasy underlying his erotic experience. The merger fantasy had a sadomasochistic structure and represented a defensive move whereby he subjugated himself to sidestep the exploration and expression of his own subjective desire. The awareness of my countertransference helped me understand this formulation, especially from the way in which I experienced his attempts to 'penetrate' me. In general, I was not excited by Michael's aggressive or more phallic presentations. Rather, it was as if his penetrations were too soft or weak. He seemed to lack substance or hardness; it was not possible for me to feel *him*.

I recognized the more primitive, narcissistic level of his manifestly sexual demand. I said, "You'd leave your desires out of it," to which he responded, "I tend not to explore my own wishes. I'd use your life to give juice to mine."

At this phase of the treatment, I understood Michael's interest in me as a substitute for his interest in himself. Along the same lines, I was aware that I did not feel a trace of erotic arousal at Michael's attempts to 'get inside me.' Rather than being excited by his interest, I felt closed in, even suffocated. There was a way in which his examination of me felt *too* in me, appropriating, as if he wanted to take me over or *become* me. To say I felt an over-dependency is not exactly right – it was as if he was trying (psychically) to *take something from me*, like the desperately starving people he had imagined clamoring at his door during the Y2K crisis.

Michael would demand that I have sex with him and insist that my refusal was sadistic, following upon what he experienced as the hypocritical, seductive analytic set-up that had trapped him in a helpless and impotent position. But beyond the sex, what did he want? He was essentially pained and furious that I would not fill up the hours with stories about my life, my experiences outside, and my desires. He felt I deprived him. He said he wanted to take my lead, to be my surrogate. I understood this as a repetition of his early, preverbal relation with his mother, one where he had to find her and empathically attune to her wishes in order to make contact, but at the expense of his own wishes. This identificatory love was a substitution of her subjectivity for his, a longing *to be her* to compensate for the inadequate strength of his own desires and longings, essentially a merger fantasy with a sadomasochistic structure.

Notes

1 In referring to the maternal, I use the terms 'mother,' 'primary caregiver,' and 'maternal' interchangeably, all of whom are not necessarily a woman. If women no longer own the feminine (Kristeva, 2019), then what I mean to convey is the way in which the infant experiences the primary caregiver's ministrations, probing and receptive to the infant's needs.

2 Noting a fear of intimacy, I hold this as an absent *capacity*, not as a prescription on how to live.

3 Likewise, Balsam (2012) argues that castration anxiety has no relevance for women, that it is a fantasy based on another fantasy, and that the pregnant body would be a natural place for the body ego.

4 Balsam's (2012) references to the female's relationship to her (potentially) pregnant body and a mature identity portrait come to mind here.

Chapter 4

The erotics of power

It is undeniable that the experience of the analysand in relation to the analyst is one of being seduced into a power relation. Though the dialectics of axes of power (and equality) are complex, erotic transferences are prone to be aroused by virtue of the many different (and in some instances orthogonal) power relations within the treatment context. A digression into the components of the treatment structure is necessary here.

Rather than aspire to the conceptually problematic (and ultimately impossible) mandates of the classical triumvirate (i.e., anonymity, neutrality, and abstinence), I find it heuristic and more phenomenally accessible to structure my psychoanalytic stance around two dimensions of the psychoanalytic project: *mutuality* and *asymmetry* (Aron, 1996; Hoffer, 1996). Indeed, these two axes are definitional of the psychoanalytic contract and it is through these two dimensions that mental and behavioral roles are assigned and guided throughout the process. *These two axes function in dialectical relation; as one is engaged, the other is deepened.* Further, this dialectic greatly intensifies the experience and longing for intimate, sexual union in the psychoanalytic context.

Foundational to the treatment contract is the background experience of *mutual, authentic engagement*. This dimension is bi-directional in the sense that there are two persons committed to working together and withstanding whatever emerges. This commitment holds out the hope for and promise of continued acceptance and understanding for the patient of even the most loathsome aspects of the self. Since the analysand is invited and encouraged to reveal areas of self-contempt and self-hatred, the promise of continued engagement in the face of these aspects of the self is simultaneously dangerous and seductive. The danger is inherent in the risk of rejection or withdrawal, despite

DOI: 10.4324/9781003391012-4

the (sometimes overt) promise of sustained commitment. The seductive aspect coincides with the universal wish to be loved totally, without judgment or merit. Though rarely actualized, the wish to be loved totally without having to give anything in return remains a lifelong wish.[1] These longings are never given up but can be set aside as life fails to fulfill them.

The seductiveness of unconditional acceptance and commitment is fueled and intensified by other fundamental and universal wishes as well. These include: (a) the desire for *unity* (to be loved totally and without separateness), (b) the desire for *purity* (to be loved without hate and unreservedly), (c) the desire for *reciprocity* (to love and be loved in return), and finally, (d) the desire for *omnipotence* (to be so powerful that one is loved by everyone everywhere at all times). All of these universals figure prominently in fantasies of romantic perfection and are stimulated in the treatment setting since the treatment contract partly instantiates their gratification. It can be said that the treatment frame both stimulates and frustrates these universal wishes which will be freighted with the analysand's historical meanings and unresolved developmental trauma. As a background experience, *these aspects of mutuality are a given* and can be considered the existential condition of being together.

The analytic context is stimulating, seductive, and frustrating for both analyst and analysand, however in very different ways due to the second dimension of the treatment context. This dimension is defined by *the asymmetric distribution of attention paid*. This axis comprises the analyst's professional and disciplined commitment to the analysand. In the psychotherapeutic and psychoanalytic setting, the treatment context is fundamentally defined by the asymmetric distribution of attention paid to the patient.

A male patient with a history of subjugation to his single mother says,

> I want to flow with my emotions for you, but it's a trap. I can flow, but I don't want to because I'm always reminded that this is not life. I want to believe it is real between us and be able to say 'she really cares about me.' I ask myself, Do I feel something personal between you and me? I would like to believe there's something flowing from you to me, but I don't trust it. Is it our purpose? Why is it relevant? Is it unprofessional? It's not our work, it's not your job. If I want to believe you care for me personally, then I'm in the analysis trap.

Chetrit-Vatine (2004) and Wilson (2013) emphasize the ethic and responsibility of the analyst's positioning in relation to the patient. Acknowledging the seduction to a one-way relationship that the analytic contract sets up, these aspects of the analyst's offer of care reside in and are implicated in the asymmetric dimension of the analytic contract, the unequal distribution of attention paid in the interaction. Most importantly, this aspect of the analytic setting is *not a given, but is asserted and re-asserted in each moment as the essential component of analytic process.*

We are used to referring to the power imbalance in treatment to mean that the therapist has it and the patient does not, but this common understanding is an oversimplication,.This axis of asymmetry is hierarchical in that it is constituted by several power relations, yet it is not straightforward or simple. It is an asymmetry that frames several power imbalances at once, each of which is ambivalently held by both patient and analyst. On the one hand, the analysand is positioned as special (and thereby of elevated status) and at the same time, in a desiring or needful state (thereby vulnerable and disempowered). The analyst, by contrast, is relatively contained in her/his need of the analysand (thereby empowered) yet also discounted in terms of the distribution of attention paid (and thereby dismissed, in terms of her/his personal needs). This asymmetry deepens and is concretized as the treatment progresses in the sense that the analyst continues to learn more about the patient while the reverse (relatively speaking) is not true. These forms of power are inherent in the structure of the setting, so neither participant necessarily feels subjectively or consciously empowered.[2]

These two axes, mutuality and asymmetry, function in dialectical relation. For example, the asymmetry deepens the analysand's need for mutual, affective engagement as a way to ameliorate the humiliating, disempowering aspects of being the continuous focus of attention. In this way, it is the facilitation and encouragement of the analysand's openness and vulnerability that makes the analyst's love and acceptance all the more important (Hoffman, 1998). Likewise, it is the extent to which the analysand reveals her/himself, especially areas of self-hatred and self-loathing, that intensifies the analyst's power in relation to the analysand. In other words, it is the analysand's self-revelations that empowers the analyst and intensifies the analysand's desire for a mutual, authentic engagement (deriving from the analysand's disempowerment).

In these ways, the treatment setting is a complex structure that uniquely instantiates several contradictions. Especially interesting is the way in which the treatment setting combines these two contradictory axes: the axis of equality and mutuality (a *we're in this together* type of experience) along with the contradictory and imbalanced focus on the analysand (a *you are in this alone* type of experience). The treatment setting is the point at which these two axes converge, creating the paradox of a simultaneous feeling of mutuality and asymmetry, of intimacy and aloneness, and of equality and hierarchy. It is a mixture of existential givens and disciplined choices. These are tensions that the analysand is persistently moved to resolve, to disequilibrate or level the hierarchy, so to speak, and to make contact with the authentic person behind the professional role.

It can be said that psychoanalysis is a process by which the analysand attempts to both empower and disempower the analyst (and vice versa) in an ongoing, increasingly more urgent way. By virtue of the special combination of mutuality and asymmetry, a tension is established that the analysand both desires and hates. This necessarily will reconstruct and recapitulate the analysand's relationship to authority and power in general. The psychoanalytic context and the analysand's experience with the analyst (given the power structures within it), is a particularly intense instantiation of this relation. Not surprisingly, in those for whom parental experiences are freighted with trauma, hypocritical, or exploitative uses and abuses of power, the analytic process will be experienced with great mistrust and skepticism.[3]

Likewise, for the analyst, there is a powerful contradiction inherent in the intersection of these two axes. For the analyst, the constant dismissal of personal need is frustrating and depleting yet the analyst is also partially gratified and titillated by the moments of attunement that the analysand offers. It might be said that *the frustration of asymmetry is counterbalanced by the seduction of mutuality and momentary attunements.* For the depleted analyst, a constant temptation is to transform *'we're in this together differently'* into a *'we're in this together the same'* perversion of the process. These vicarious identifications evoke and temporarily unsettle the analyst as she or he decenters and resonates with the analysand's experience. Recentering and thereby re-asserting separateness and difference are crucial aspects of this fluctuating dialectic that can become more muted, less sharp, and only half-heartedly asserted over time.

This is the nature and paradox of the psychoanalytic stance. There is the fluctuation of regressive and progressive emotional resonances, the inherent structured power imbalances, and the dynamic, resistive pressures to level the hierarchy from both within and without, i.e., from within ourselves and from the patient. Psychoanalytic therapies take place within a highly seductive and potentially intimate context of *asymmetry* – this potentially depleting and titillating structure makes external supports and gratifications for the analyst, specifically sources of intimacy, crucial bases of recalibration and equilibrium. The asymmetry, a complicated cross-current of deprivations for both analyst and analysand, is ambivalently held throughout the process. Both analyst and analysand are moved to disequilibrate, dismantle, and simplify the engagement often yielding to the constant temptation of *mutuality*.

MICHAEL: The aggressivization of the erotic transference

In the middle phase of Michael's analysis,[4] I noticed a welcome shift in my countertransference. Michael had become more appealing. His more differentiated presence allowed me greater room to breathe and to see him from a crucial distance which, paradoxically, made intimacy possible. At the same time, his hostility seemed to intensify and I was aware of an increasing discomfort in me.

Michael said, "I think I'm sexually competent. But what do women want? I think women want to be raped. A void to be filled. Women like men to be strong. An 'I'm taking you,' Tony Soprano kind of thing. But technique is a question – how long, what to touch, how to touch." I said, "You have a lot of curiosity about who wants what, sexually, aggressively ..." to which he responded, "I don't want to be a man that doesn't regulate, modulate, control." I said, "How to feel your thrust, fill your own void, and at the same time give a woman what she wants?" He went on, "You make it sound as if it's okay to use force. I don't know if I feel that. Maybe I do. It's a man thing. You want me to be a man." I said, "In whatever way you define that."[5]

In his outside life, Michael began to see prostitutes. Very high-priced 'escorts' about whom I learned a lot. I learned, for example, that if you pay extra, they will do 'the girlfriend thing.' This is a kind of play where they will pretend that they like you. At the same time, they seemed genuinely interested in Michael's struggles with impotence. He would openly tell them how he could not stay hard, hoping they might help him, and they were more than willing to try. Though his impotence persisted through these years, Michael became a more experienced sexual partner, especially in relation to erotically pleasuring a woman. One day, Michael came into his session and said, "Your fees are low." He continued, "Your fees are low because your services are limited."

In the third year of analysis, Michael began to express his longings in a more explicitly hostile way. This was first expressed masochistically: he wanted me to hurt and reject him in ways that both punished him and, in a fantasied way, would transform his loving feelings toward me into hate. Suicidality became a constant feature. On one occasion, Michael said,

> I'm worried I'm getting into a kind of frenzy. A crazy, negative state. I want you to tell me that you won't kiss me, you won't touch me, you won't have sexual intercourse with me. I want you to hurt me. I want you to help me turn off this primitive part of me. I want to fall into a zone of anger and destruction. I want to get angry with you. I want to harden my heart to you.

At this juncture, I understood Michael's increasing suicidality as an aggressivization of the erotic transference, initially directed inward in a defensive effort to give him the illusion of strength (hardening himself) in relation to me. The more he could take, the stronger he might feel. The more I hurt him, the more monstrous I became. He asked, "Do you take pleasure in your success at not telling me things about you? It is skillful." To which I responded, "You think I take pleasure in the very thing that causes you pain." He said,

> Yes, it is a thrill for you that you can use your skill to help me with the pain you cause... You should say rejecting things to me! I would feel bad at first, but I need to get closure. I want to be indifferent to you. I want to fall out of love with you ... Love is a humiliation.

Over time, there was an accentuated shift from masochistic to more outwardly directed aggression. This shift brought with it a set of feelings that were, to Michael, less emasculating, less subjugated, and internally strengthening, yet more threatening to me. On one occasion, he said,

> I want to show you my best self. If I wanted, I could do that, but I would be holding back. I can be mean, vicious, sarcastic. It's enticing, because a part of me doesn't want to make myself attractive to you. I can let it fly. I can attack you.

I welcomed (at least I tried to!) the emerging negative transference and expected that as Michael's aggression surfaced and was expressed more directly toward me, my challenge would be to receive it without retaliating. I hoped too that we would see a diminishment of his suicidality and self-destructive wishes, along with a strengthened sense of inner presence as he became increasingly comfortable with his aggression.

As the work progressed, many treatment goals were indeed accomplished. Michael expanded his social world, both in terms of broadening his friendships and deepening his engagement with a new girlfriend. He took greater pleasure in his academic achievements and displayed more confidence at work, e.g., incorporating humor in his papers and presentations. There were some developments in my countertransference as well. For one, I was aware of experiencing Michael as more appealing. I felt less closed in and suffocated, as if his more differentiated presence allowed me more space to relax in his presence.

Michael then revealed a murderous, vengeful fantasy about me that he said had been in his mind a year earlier. He said, "I want you to hurt the way I do. I want things to go wrong in your life. I want you to feel similar pain." Momentarily retreating from his attack, I restated his wish and said, "You want me to understand." He corrected me, "No, I want your marriage to go bad." I felt a bit rattled at the intensity of his hostility. Lamely, I responded, "You want me to feel your pain." He nodded. I continued, "You want what you think I have, but you feel hopeless to get it for yourself. So you want to destroy it in me. This is envy." He then said,

> Yes, surely. I feel violent toward you. It's a temporary pleasure too. If I say I want to kill you, it's not a friendly thing to say. If I kill you, then I'll have to kill myself. It's a logistical necessity. I've thought of this several times. Pills are not a definitive way to kill myself. Most men kill themselves with a gun. I don't have a gun now."

Bracing myself against how frightened I was becoming, I pursued these thoughts further. I said, "And killing me?" Michael responded,

I thought of stabbing you. That is metaphoric. A gun is fast, decisive. But it's just killing. A knife is more expressive. It links to feelings. More cathartic. It releases what you feel. It's prolonged. More interactive. You'd say something. I'd have to deal with that. You'd scream.

I imagine now that Michael could sense the increased adrenaline in the atmosphere. He became interested in my reaction. He asked, "What are you thinking? I need to know."

I was aware of being frightened and began wondering whether the treatment was proving to be harmful for Michael (and possibly me). I wondered if Michael was able to withstand the feelings (especially envious and vengeful feelings) aroused in the process of uncovering his desires. Perhaps I had overestimated his capacities to tolerate the frustrating effects of the treatment. I also wondered if the treatment structure itself had evaporated in Michael's mind, devolving into a basic and personal rejection of him by me. It was becoming clear to me that the tension between the professional and the personal relationship had collapsed (at least for me), and I did not know if it could be reestablished. Most prominent in my mind, I could not ignore the memory of his buying a gun just a few years prior. It occurred to me that perhaps this was the threat some female analysts might want to foreclose.

In the moment, I thought Michael needed to see his effect on me to counter the utter helplessness that cut across his humiliation, envy, and feelings of rejection. I also needed to find a way to reestablish a safe structure around our work. So I responded from a personal level, disclosing my concerns. I told Michael I was frightened and that I felt threatened. Then I said,

I am worried maybe you can't handle the feelings that are being stirred up. Still, I believe putting all this into words is important. You want to communicate … you want me to understand the pain you're in and that's what killing with a knife would do. And you want to have a reaction from me.

He responded at first in a dismissive manner, but then demonstrated an ability to reflect on what I had said. He said, "Oh, here we go with my mother," but then added, "It did come to my mind too, though, the way I felt trapped and unable to get anything from her. She never understood how I felt. I was some kind of surrogate to her. But there's also something about envy. I'll never have what you have." I said, "So you'd rather no one have it, than I have it and not you." He said, "Yes, that's the feeling." I continued, "So, for a moment, you can believe there's nothing you're missing." He said, "You think knowing your desires, feeling your desires is a great big help. A great big step for mankind." To which I responded, "Yes, I do. But I know it's painful to realize what you want, especially if you feel hopeless about getting these things for yourself." He said, "In my real life, I am hopeless, but with you, if I stabbed you, there would at least be one minute when *you* needed *me*."

I then turned to the moment in Michael's fantasy where "I would say something." Exploration of this did not reveal a specific statement but rather an experience where I would plead with him. He said he wanted to see my need of him and see me be as utterly helpless as he was as a child.

I don't remember how the session ended and I have no memory of him leaving the office. I immediately took verbatim notes.

Not surprisingly, I felt an immediate need for a consultation. I checked my appointment book and noticed a fortuitous coincidence of timing – the next meeting of my peer supervision group was to occur in just a few days. As it happened, I had been presenting Michael and was scheduled to continue.

And then I did one more thing, another step in the enactment. I told my husband. I did not identify Michael, but I read the notes from the session to my husband. My husband is not an analyst or therapist, but it helped to have him behind me, at least in my mind. I wish at the time I had thought of asking him to stay home for a few days while I faced Michael for his upcoming sessions, but neither of us thought of this. I braced myself for the next several days.

In the next session and for the remainder of the week, Michael expressed enormous regret at the "insane, awful things" he had said, referring specifically to the fantasy of killing me. He insisted this was not a current preoccupation. He said that he was simply remembering these fantasies from a year ago. Of course, this did not help. Even if I took his words at face value, I was not comforted by the thought that these fantasies were no longer operative on some level. I was afraid that he might not be telling me the truth or that he might not know the extent to which he could be overcome with murderous impulses at any time. I felt somewhat reassured that Michael was remorseful, but I did not know to what extent he or I were in safe territory. Though

I believed it was best for him to verbalize his thoughts and wishes, it was undeniable that we had lost the feeling of playfulness between us.

For the next three weeks, (an eternity!) I remained terrified. Given I had a home office, he knew where I lived and though we did not live in the same town, images of him stalking me kept intruding into my mind. I never saw him. But this is how frightened I was. I wanted to involve others and decided I would, but I also worried that it might be too late. There was a dreadful feeling that this was now between him and me on a personal level, that the treatment frame had been irrevocably lost and that it would not matter what steps I might take.

I then discussed this vignette with a colleague who shared an anecdote involving a similar clinical challenge experienced by a colleague of hers. When this colleague discussed her case with a supervisor, he purportedly said, "Don't worry – these things don't usually happen." That did not help either!

I looked over my process notes of our work from the prior year. I came across Michael's words as he described lovesick images of himself as "a man lurching around" with "sensual stabs in my heart." I realized the fantasy of stabbing me represented these feelings and noted the phrase "sensual stabs" as expressing an aggressive penetration.

Michael continued to express regret at frightening me and a grave concern that I would decide I could no longer work with him. He worried that even if we continued, I would now see him as crazy or a "pathological threat" and no longer hold him in a respectful light. He was afraid he had destroyed something between us and that I disliked him intensely. Though I did not state anything of the sort, I did notice I had become very constricted in my manner. I knew my anxiety was apparent to him.

In the immediate aftermath, I felt a need to ground our discussion in a framework of concrete safety. I asked Michael if he could gauge the relative weight of fantasy versus action in what he had said. He responded that it was "way into the fantasy camp. The reality is I don't have the courage even to commit suicide, even though I talk about it a lot." He then offered several examples of his pacifist nature, citing a lifetime of inhibition in many realms. Still, images of old ladies feeding arsenic to unsuspecting strangers plagued me. On a more realistic level, I could not forget that he had previously bought a gun.

I presented Michael to my peer group, which proved essential in reestablishing my own sense of balance. The reactions and thoughts of individual members spanned the full range of formulations.

One member thought this was no different from treating his suicidality, another thought Michael was more primitive and action-prone than I was appreciating and the third felt cautiously optimistic. Rather than being confused or frustrated by the contradictions, I found myself welcoming the differences. I wanted to hold a variety of dialogues along different pathways and I also knew any single formulation of the case would have been unconvincing.

Then I did one more thing – a final step in the enactment. I disclosed to Michael that I had presented the material to my peer supervision group and that I would continue to do so for some time. I knew my disclosure was a direct result of my residual feeling of threat and an attempt to reestablish safety for myself.

At the time, Michael was visibly relieved by my disclosure and he said, "Oh really! What did they say?" By such a reaction, I took it that Michael was clearly displaying his assumption that this was a way to get more help. I had the fantasy that the group served a paternal function, a third vertex, a symbol of the protective and corrective influence of the analytic community for both Michael and me. I immediately relaxed. I could see that Michael *was interested again in his mind*, not in destroying me or himself. Not only was it essential to have the support for myself, but the ability to bring the peer group's presence and superego into the treatment served to counterbalance the dyadically organized closed system (like him and his mother) we seemed to be viciously re-creating. Through our subsequent discussions, Michael and I have also recognized a repetition of bringing in superego figures, much like his turning his gun over to the police. The need for a third presence, an overseeing body, a limit, a vertex establishing a triangle, or at least a father figure are all meanings we explored.

The crux of these developments culminating in the fantasy to murder me, the stabbing fantasy, was unmistakeably orgasmic in nature. In Michael's fantasy, I plead with him in a lurching, bloody state of passion. In my countertransference experience, I cannot say it turned me on, however it did intensely grip me so that I could not think of anyone or anything else except him for what seemed to me like a very long period of time. I believe this was an unconscious function and wish of the fantasy itself.

Michael stirred me up so much, I needed others to calm me down. I got consultation from various 'thirds' – all 'phallic' figures (though not all male) to fortify my intimidated self. It can be said that not only did the dyad need a third, not only did Michael need a father, but also I needed a 'so-called man.' What was this movement in the analytic field and how did it connect with the erotic dimension of the treatment?

I had wanted to engage the man in Michael and facilitate his emergence. In so doing, Michael's aggression came through in full force; perhaps the man in Michael then needed to make contact with the man in me. Counterbalancing the feminine with the so-called masculine aspects of our role, we both needed more phallus – Michael had not wanted to experience me as an empowered, phallic woman earlier in the treatment because of its subjugating effects on him and I too resisted access to the male in me. It took a third to say, "Yes, we want to kill the person who humiliates and rejects us. More than that, you want to make me spill my guts the way you feel you have done with me." A third, a man, and the man in me.

As his analysis continued, Michael transformed in his ability to erotically excite me. Not that this was at the forefront all the time, but I did find myself imagining living with him, being his lover, and identifying with the women in his life. Non-pressured erotic musings emerged along with the full range of everyday concordant and complementary affective experiences. Michael had become whole.

Michael began dating more vigorously. He went online and met some women through a dating site. One of the women was a particularly vibrant, affectionate, and emotional woman who he began dating seriously. The first time they had sexual relations, he was able to penetrate her and feel the full strength of his desires without fear. He was able to use his thrust inside her without worrying he might kill her. (Perhaps like he had penetrated me.)

I won an award for this treatment and in an ironic twist, I received the award on the same day Michael married his new beloved.

JULIA: Facing her beloved

The case of Julia (also presented in the prior chapter) illustrates the development of internal capacities through the early phase of analysis and a new development as her strengthened subjectivity allowed for triangular relations. Julia had terminated her analysis after five years, having experienced increased feelings of inner strength, confidence in displaying and selling her work, and the ability to sustain romantic and sexual feelings in a monogamous relationship.[6] She was able to be more assertive in her goals and displayed greater enjoyment the intensity of her passion. Her depression had lifted and she left treatment feeling substantially strengthened.

Subsequently, after a year and a half, Julia returned. She acknowledged lasting changes from the analysis, yet a reticence to 'take the spotlight' still lingered and she wanted to continue to explore this inhibition. She also expressed discomfort at continuing with a reduced fee (though I thought she still needed one). We decided to reduce the number of sessions, thereby raising the fee per hour (though still at a reduced rate). She also chose to sit up. I had the fantasy that she wanted to *face me more as an equal*. We proceeded with a face-to-face treatment for the next year and a half, mostly exploring her feelings while exhibiting her work.

During one hour, Julia was describing the feeling of hanging her paintings for a show, the moment when people begin to arrive and gaze at her work, a moment when she sometimes catches someone's eye. She described this moment as derailing her. She wondered about an earlier interpretation of her unconscious fantasy that "no one was there," the fantasy that the person looking might not see her or her work. We speculated that perhaps this fantasy functioned in part as a wish, a protection from the potentially derailing connection to a particular other. (I was reminded of my own experience presenting papers at conferences where I feel less anxious peering out to a group of anonymous faces as opposed to the self-conscious feeling when someone I know is in the audience.)

This formulation was consistent with the ease with which Julia used the couch from the beginning, perhaps to protect her from the potentially derailing awareness of *a particular other*. Now we wondered if being *alone in a crowd* represented both a fear and a protection: the fear of abandonment as we had initially understood as well as a protection against the awareness of a knowing, particular other. Her use of the couch and the chair elaborated both sides of this dialectic wherein safety, initially residing in a more diffuse type of engagement (like her sexual relations with multiple partners), was optimally experienced at a distance (i.e., on the couch). The couch protected her from the potentially disjunctive experience of my separateness and the complexity of my internal world (for her, as we would later discover, my potential as a competitor and object of envy).

In this later phase of analysis (sitting up), Julia's associations began to revolve around my external appearance. (We look and are about the same age.) She would comment on my body, weight, and hair. She referred to my style of clothing, comparing her "funky, natural, and un-conventional" taste with my more professional, "less risky" appearance. In particular, she disliked my suit jackets, saying I dressed in an uncrea-tive, consumer-driven fashion. She said she could not dress the way I do because the arts required more flamboyance. I told her I thought she wanted to compare herself to me in order to find her own style. She spoke of memories of her mother repairing her older sisters' cloth-ing and handing them down to her. She said she always wanted new clothing but there was not enough money. She admitted she still felt "not dressed up enough" and asked if I would view a video of a recent show with an eye on her outfits. I told her it sounded like she wanted feedback on her appearance, especially for showings of her work. She mentioned acting coaches who help performers with their stage outfits and wondered if she could find a similar person for an art showing. She added, "I've always disparaged that form of help as a waste of money, but I think I can tolerate someone examining me now." The analogy to this phase of treatment, where I looked directly at her, was obvious. Soon after, she hired such a coach. In her analysis, we focused instead on her competitive and envious feelings that were beginning to emerge.

Julia began to incorporate attention to her physical (external) ap-pearance as part of her performance art. She gradually came to tolerate the previously denied and unwanted reality that *the way she appeared* in the spotlight was part of her anxiety and fear of competition. She associated to her body as too big, too hungry, but also as an exterior container for her inner desires. I recognized her increasing capacity to tolerate competitive and envious feelings toward me based on her experience of both my inner and outer self.

The earlier wish to be inside my skin (or me in hers) now took on a different meaning in the *après coup* of the analytic process. Whereas in the early phases of the analysis Julia wanted a feeling of merger with me, thereby bypassing my exteriority or separateness, she now gazed at me from a distance and imagined my inner life. She fantasized that I was internally powerful and strong yet worried that she was impov-erishing me through the reduced fee. Omnipotent fantasies associated with her aggression emerged in competitive and envious forms. Would she tire me out or make me hate her? Would I envy her as she became strong? Was being strong the same as being too big or hungry? Was there enough in me to give to her along with my other patients? *Alone in a crowd* was transformed again, revealing another layer of meaning – she wanted to be my *one and only* among the crowd of my patients.

Notes

1 See, for example, S. Smith's (1977) discussion of *The Golden Fantasy*.
2 See Essay 10, *The nature of boundaries*, and Essay 13, *The art of the boundary* (in Celenza, 2022a).
3 For a more elaborated discussion of the power dimensions of the analytic process, see Celenza (2007).
4 See Chapter 3 for the early phases of Michael's analysis.
5 Though the defining reach of gender is currently undergoing radical transformation [see Dimen, 2003; Harris, 2005; and Saketopoulou and Pellegrini (2023) for vibrant discussions], Michael's personal struggle to "feel more male" coincided with traditional stereotypes of masculinity and femininity.
6 Again, this is not prescriptive but indicative of a capacity, should she choose to live this way.

Chapter 5

Are erotic transferences gendered?

Does gender or anatomical sex affect the experience and expression of erotic transferences? I pose this question in this manner, with this specific phraseology because it is the way it is most often posed to me. But in order to answer this query, it needs to be translated into several, more carefully considered questions:

1　Are erotic transferences as emergent phenomena sexed and/or gendered in some *a priori* way?
2　Furthering the above question, are the different types of erotic transferences sexed and/or gendered in different yet specific ways?
3　Does the sex and/or gender of the analyst matter, in the sense of influencing the emergence and types of erotic transferences that may develop?
4　Does the sex and/or gender of the analysand influence the ways erotic transferences might express themselves?

Before exploring these questions more specifically, it is important to take a step back and elaborate the assumptions upon which the following assertions rest. As in all of my writings, I presume psychic multi-sexualities and multi-gendered psychic realities. These reside at the level of potentials and are not necessarily lived out, although with any one individual, these psychic realities may have more or less presence in material reality (Celenza, 2000, 2010, 2012, 2014, 2022a,b; see also Perelberg, 2018).[1] As you can see, it is important to make a firm distinction between psychic and material realities when considering these questions. Neither level can be disregarded, the two may not align, and it is psychic reality that will structure and determine the ways in which

DOI: 10.4324/9781003391012-5

material reality is experienced. It is psychic reality that is represented in all transferences.

Since erotic transferences, through the channel of libidinal urges, express ways in which the analysand currently processes her/his embodied desires, we must acknowledge that the psychic realities of sex and/or gendered internalizations are intertwined with erotic transferences at every level. Conscious, preconscious, and unconscious experience of one's bodily and erotic urges will be implicated and, as noted, these may not align with material reality. Nor will the sex and/or gender(s) of each member of the dyad necessarily align with the conscious or unconscious experience of the other or with the psychic fantasies of each other. Still, all of these domains are relevant and will become arenas for psychoanalytic exploration.

These sexed and gendered experiences and expressions intertwine and define an individual's erotic experience and erotic identity. These can be expressed metaphorically in many ways, but fundamentally define and are encapsulated by sexed and gendered experience. It is my contention that the various sexed and gendered binaries should be transcended to culminate in a multiplicity within (see also Goldner, 1991; Elise, 1998; Balsam, 2001). As I have written elsewhere (Celenza, 2014):

> [F]rom within the position of the experiencing self (the experiencer/agent or embodied subject), individual experience can be described as some amalgam of *receptivity and potency* – in the language of sexuality, *holding and penetration* or, in the language of the body, *openness and backbone*. Put as a more traditional stereotype: the feminine and masculine, but here representing bi-gendered aspects of the self as opposed to one over the other. Indeed, to describe phenomenal experience form the position of the embodied subject, I am describing this dialectic, the experiencer/agent as a position where one has achieved some blend of access to feeling (*receptivity*) and articulated selfhood (*potency*) . . . the vision of the self in an inclusive and gendered multiplicity . . .
>
> My aim is to engage this polarity (receptivity and potency), stereotypically definitional of femininity and masculinity, in order to expose this polarity as a false dichotomy, the poles of which are not actually opposite (thereby are not mutually exclusive) in any register of meaning. These reckonings ... vary intra-individually as relational patterns shift and self-experience multiplies and

expands. *Most importantly, I view these poles as liberated from any hierarchical power relation, in that neither pole is privileged,* though in any particular individual one may be. ...

As treatment progresses, it becomes possible to transcend cultural stereotypes (of gender, race, ethnicity, age, etc.) . . . This expansion involves the acceptance and inclusion of binarial, oppositional categories in a 'both/and' multiplicity, in effect to achieve a *unique gender blend.*

(pp. 4–6)

In the previous two chapters, I presented case examples of erotic transferences that developed in the context of long-term analyses with a cis-female (Julia) and cis-male (Michael) analysand. As was evident in the two case descriptions, questions about the body, its erotic desires and functioning, femininity, and masculinity were all central in the psychic meanings that were being explored throughout the analyses. In addition, the structure, shape, fantasies, and meanings of the erotic transferences undergoing development within these analyses changed in fundamental yet meaningful ways through the course of the analyses. Though each individual identified as cis-gendered and heterosexual, questions as to the nature of their bodies and sexual orientation arose (though not necessarily presented fully in these chapters) and were part of their psychoanalytic journies. The journey along which we accompany our analysands can take many twists and turns; sexualities and gendered internalizations will arise with uncertain and individualized trajectories. Therefore, to ask if erotic transferences are sexed and/or gendered is to ask if the anatomical sex or gender(s) of a person is meaningful to a person's identity and psychoanalytic process. The answer can only be "of course." In my view, this answers the first question: are erotic transferences sexed and/or gendered and here the answer is definitively yes, but not in predictable, stereotyped, or *a priori* ways. There is nothing *a priori* about these emergences, i.e., before individualized experience is interpreted by the individual (consciously or unconsciously).[2] *Erotic transferences are unconsciously structured by highly individualized psychic fantasies of anatomical sex and gender(s) that do not necessarily align with material reality.* Another way to state this is that *erotic transferences are structured according to sexed and gendered themes at the level of psychic reality but not at the level of material reality.*

This brings me to the next question as to whether different types of erotic transferences coincide with specific sexed and/or gendered themes (e.g., are maternal erotic transferences about women?). As stated in all of the previous chapters, I have referred to maternality as liberated from the presumed anatomical sex and/or gender(s) of the primary caregiver. Therefore, it is reasonable to state that maternal erotic transferences are not necessarily structured by female bodies or femininity *in material reality*, though the psychic fantasies of any one person will construct and define each of these according to the nature and experience of their early infancy on conscious and unconscious levels. These, then, will come to define the maternal and femininity, whether or not the primary caregiver was an anatomically-sexed woman. Our language is drenched in gender so 'femininity,' as we commonly refer to it, will come to be defined by early maternal experiences despite the primary caregiver being an anatomically-sexed man. Thus, at the level of psychic reality (and to answer the second question succinctly), erotic transferences are not specifically or *a priori* sexed or gendered, though any one individual will construct their personal idioms revolving around sexed and gendered themes, shaping erotic transferences. To be clear, maternal erotic transferences are not predetermined to be about women, femaleness, or femininity in an *a priori* way, however these will come to define womanhood and/or femininity for any particular individual, even if the individual's primary caregiver was a man. Again, it is the sexed and gendered themes of *psychic reality* that determine the nature and type of erotic transferences, not those of material reality.

This brings me to the next set of questions revolving around the anatomical sex and gender(s) of both analyst and analysand. Here, we must specify on what level we are intending to answer these questions. Is the anatomical sex of either member of the dyad consequential and does the anatomical and/or gender(s) of the analyst predetermine or influence the construction of an erotic transference? In the past, I was fond of answering this question with an aphorism, "The anatomical sex and/or gender(s) of the analyst in relation to the analysand is important for the alliance but not for the transference." This aphorism oversimplifies complex phenomena by placing them into neat categories, that do not hold (after all, transferences structure *all* relations, including the alliance). Yet, at a conscious, phenomenal level, this aphorism may be a useful guiding principle. To translate the aphorism more precisely, *the conscious experience* of the sex and/or gender(s) of the analyst is important for the alliance but not for the transference.

In the first vignettes of Julia and Michael (Chapter 3), the phases of each analysis were characterized by an early maternal erotic transference. In the subsequent vignettes (Chapter 4), each developed within the analyses oedipal-level rivalries of integration of aggression for each person (in highly individualized ways). One point among many that the choice of these cases illustrates is that erotic transferences are, by and large, *not sexed or gendered by material reality.* Both persons reckoned with questions relevant to maternal erotic transferences and oedipal-level rivalries in their own individualized way. Maternal and paternal transferences emerged despite my being a cis-gendered woman and their being cis-gendered female or male (respectively). These transferences were determined by sexed and gendered themes in their *psychic realities* that did or did not align with material reality. In addition, the individualized psychic fantasies for each of them changed over the course of their analyses, further illustrating that erotic transferences are not sexed or gendered in *a priori*, material ways.

Despite the emphasis on the individualized nature of the psychic fantasies that emerge in any analysis, there are universal challenges in the development of subjectivity and especially in becoming a *subject of desire* (or desiring subject, see Harkless, 2023) confronting all persons. These universal challenges, each processed, embodied, and enlivened in highly individualized ways, include (but are not limited to): the crisis of separateness, the reckoning with difference, and the threat of the intentionality of the other. They emerge in early maternal erotic transferences and the psychic realities of sexed and gendered themes will play a role. The experience and tolerance of triangular relations (competition, rivalry, and envy) as well as the ability to harness one's potency while remaining receptive to and capable of surrendering to desire are also universal challenges that are not sexed or gendered in some *a priori* or stereotyped way, but which will be constructed and intertwined with sexed and gendered themes for any one individual as psychic realities continually structure and elaborate them. All of these challenges vary across individuals and must be reckoned with regardless of the material reality of anatomical sex and/or gender(s), including the anatomical sex and gender(s) of the primary caregiver/analyst.

When the primary caregiver/analyst and child/analysand are of the same anatomical sex and gender (as phenomenally experienced in material reality), however, there can be intensifications of early developmental imperatives revolving around sameness and merger wishes. These can be seen easily at a strictly phenomenal level since the bodies of each share anatomical similarity. Another speculation that may be involved revolves around the supposition that females have more fluid boundaries than do males. For example, Stotland (1969) observed that female infants more readily cry upon hearing another infant cry, reflecting perhaps a greater inborn capacity for empathy among females. Along with this is a mother's projection of her own enigmatic sexuality into her daughter's psyche (Laplanche, 1989, 1997; Scarfone, 2015, 2023) that may be based on the presumption of sameness and unconscious merger wishes, again, suggesting greater fluidity in boundaries between mother and daughter. Irigaray[3] artfully speaks of this: "The girl has the mother ... in her skin, in the humidity of the mucous membranes, in the intimacy of her most intimate parts, in the mystery of her relation to gestation, birth and to her sexual identity."

In summary, it is the *psychic realities* of sexed and gendered internalizations that will structure erotic transferences. These are not inborn, inherent, or determined in *a priori* or stereotyped ways but are highly individualized and may change and become further elaborated as the individual grows through life. Material reality does not structure transferences but may influence the way others experience us. For example, intensifications based on outward similarity or difference in phenomenal, material reality may influence the construction of erotic transferences.

Maternal[4] eroticism as vitalizing

Regardless of sex or gender(s) on a material level, it is through body-based ministrations and the primary caregiver's empathic recognition and love that the maternal figure initiates and for a time, comprises the baby's entire relation to the world. From an intersubjective perspective, then, *the first signifier[5] of the erotic* is derived from the infant's experience of its body as held, touched, gazed at, stimulated, soothed, frustrated, and rejected by the maternal figure, the primary caregiver, and this experience is not *a priori* gendered.

Kristeva describes the experience (and state) of maternal eroticism (or, as she terms it, reliance), as at once a *vitalizing* passionate vocation, a *de-vitalizing* (separating or discharging) force, including associations with the *abject*, and a tenacious, *re-vitalizing* instinct.

Kristeva (2014a, b) describes maternal eroticism as a *vitalizing*, passionate vocation that holds, links, binds, adheres to, and is committed to the life of the child. It lives in a paradoxical frontier where "a consciousness emerges into the "psychic revolution of materiality"..." (p. 75), in the space between subject/object, where "the Thing is delivered from its state of Thingness and [it] releases another living subject to the world" (pp. 75–76). To provide these components with a real-world grounding, we can see the vitalizing energy a mother offers her infant (on both psychic and bodily levels) in the invitation *to be*, through being delivered, seen, and touched. Instinctively, the good-enough mother (Winnicott, 1960) says to her infant some version of "Hello! Yes! I see you!" in a reflexive, lilting, high-pitched tone, all the while stroking, physically holding, and rhythmically soothing her baby. This is the mother's invitation *to be* as well as *to have (her)* as an object of love. She invites the baby's presence as both body and being, (however undifferentiated and nascent).

None of these ministrations and interactions need be consciously sexed or gendered, however the mother does have as yet untranslated messages that she unconsciously transmits to the infant (even before the infant is born). This is the conscious and unconscious seduction by the mother, with all its excitations and inflections, the mother's enigmatic messages conveyed in the chora's sensory surround (especially from her body) through *touch, gaze, and tonalities*. The baby 'takes in' the mother even when the mother transmits mixed messages, perhaps does *not* invite the baby in, or obstructs and frustrates the baby's seeking, pleas, needs, and demands.

The mother is a complex *bodily* force to the baby, mysterious and erotic, serving as a launching pad for seeking closeness with or being repelled by others.

> The body [of the other] is *enigmatic* ... it is connected with [a] personal life and is like the habitat in which the human being seeks closeness and union with others ... corporeality ... [it is] our surface of contact with being.
>
> (see Merleau-Ponty, 1964/1945, p. 229; cited in Moya and Lorrain, 2016, pp. 744–745, *italics added*)

The baby's complex experience with the mother's body will be internalized and bear its imprint, referenced as a template for experience with others throughout life.

Maternal eroticism as de-vitalizing

Kristeva (2014a, b) reminds us that maternal eroticism is also *de-vitalizing* as the mother separates and 'discharges.' The mother is a mother who can say 'no,' i.e., maternal eroticism includes the mother who separates, absents herself, and causes the baby to confront loss. In these ways, Kristeva notes that maternal eroticism is also fragile in the sense that it can be invaded, frustrated, obstructed, and reduced, *devitalized* by the work of the death drive. After all, the baby is originally ejected through the violence of labor where the mother risks her and her baby's lives.

Yet, it is a momentous gift from the mother to the baby, when the mother *ejects* the baby from her body, creating a separation between them but also giving the baby its life in the world. The baby is vulnerable to the mother's misattunement, frustration, and obstruction and in these ways, the life and death components of maternal eroticism *function in dialectical relation*. It is through the forces of separation, frustration, disappointment, absence, and loss within maternal eroticism that the baby and child are vitalized, just as through absence, the child is able to think, create, play, and, thereby constitute itself. As Balsam (2014) notes, "[W]e must *abject* the maternal, Kristeva says, the object which has created us, in order to construct an identity" (p. 95).

In both its vitalizing (binding) and devitalizing (unbinding) components, then, (especially in tolerable measure), maternal eroticism *dialectically* conveys, communicates, and offers the child experiences that promote its thinking, creativity, and its own erotic capacities. It is through identification with her lust for life, her potential destructiveness and frustrating potential, along with the challenges of separateness that the mother *transmits* to her baby *its own* lust for life and anxieties or dreads for life's challenges.

The work of the abject in de-vitalizing maternal eroticism

Prolonged or traumatic experiences of separateness, absence, and loss can create a sense of emptiness, a dreaded void, or deadness, what Kristeva (1980, 2014a, b) coins *the abject*.[6] For Kristeva, normal developmental challenges, if traumatic, may "manifest in paroxysmal disasters of ..... abjection ... a "normal" psychosexual element of maternal eroticism" (Kristeva, 2014a, p. 76). "Maternal eroticism renders

... the life and death drives both problematic and available, and places them together in the service of living as an 'open structure'" (2014a, p. 71).

Kristeva locates these experiences in the mother's body. The abject is prelinguistic, an almost reflex reaction to all that is disowned or repulsed by the psyche. The theory of abjection "concerns disgusting and horrific materials ... representing unmentionable elements of the self that are vigorously to be kept subliminal [Kristeva, 1980] ... death infecting life" (Balsam, 2014, p. 94).

The abject can be concretized through their association with familiar extruded, but representable objects (e.g., blood, germs, guts, feces, and vomit). These concrete phobic objects can be used as displacements for abject traumatic experiences that then come under one's fantasied omnipotent control. Parts of the mother's body (e.g., genes, blood, guts, vagina[7,8]) as well as associated psychological and behavioral ministrations (e.g., her gaze, touch, or voice), as concretized displacement objects, can, thereby, be psychologically managed, i.e., phobically avoided, controlled, or even fetishized.

Here, Green's (1986, 1999) work of the negative[9] and Winnicott's (1960, 1971) failure of transitional phenomena are relevant to Kristeva's 'work of the abject' as the child experiences various kinds of psychic spaces that *foreclose* the capacity to think and play. The work of the negative, in its double meaning of (on one pole), a fertile, receptive transitional space (as in Winnicott) and on the other pole, a foreclosed void, is consistent with the dual aspects of maternal eroticism, the life and death drives, respectively.

There are a variety of intriguing clinical and theoretical understandings that address the de-erotization of maternal signifiers in particular, especially as these are tied to conscious and unconscious experience. Wilson (2014) notes the lack of theorizing in the realm of the maternal and calls it a "shrinking of effort ... in the face of the [Lacanian] *real*, especially of the real as flesh, the feminine, the maternal" (p. 105). The mother is the mother of primary union, fundamental difference (to my reading, prior to sexual or gender categories) and in the face of the specter of death. We reflexively turn away from frightening, horrific aspects of life that resist symbolization.

We could extend Winnicott's and Green's visual-spatial metaphors of different types of psychic spaces, placed on a continuum, and integrate this metaphor with the work of the abject. Functioning as a verb and because of its frightening, horrific nature, the work of the abject can be defensively concretized, so that repellant objects can be phobically avoided, i.e., psychically managed as the abject comes under fantasied omnipotent control. By extension, then, it is in the foreclosed void of the negative, visualized as *the imploding force of a black hole wherein signifiers of the abject do their de-vitalizing work.*

The fear of the abject, unconsciously located in the mother's body, can make the confrontation with the mother *as a desired object of internalization* a tremendous threat, the mother's body becoming the site of problematic signifiers of the abject. Both the desire of the child to *take in* the mother and the mother's ability *to give herself to* her child, *i.e., to transmit* are processes that can come to represent unconscious encounters with potential threats or even death. In these ways, desire for the mother can become de-vitalized, defensively disowned, or even deadened.

Because of its fragility as an open system, Kristeva implies (and Balsam [2014] directly asserts) that it is the theory of the abject that explains the erasure of "fecund femaleness" (Balsam, 2014, p. 94). We could say that maternal eroticism is *prone to de-eroticization* by carrying within it the seeds of its own destruction. This may be especially true if/when the work of the abject diminishes or outright deadens affective (including erotic and sexual) experience.

Re-vitalization in maternal eroticism

Kristeva (2014a, b) describes yet another component of maternal eroticism, the revitalizing component, as the mother who *suffers* and *endures*. The mother can recapture the child's bereft fall into the void in her reunion and repair with the child, thereby *re-vitalizing* experiences of separateness, loss, and absence. In her fierce "refusal to collapse" (Kristeva, 2014a, p. 77), maternal eroticism endures and tenaciously holds up the vitalizing components of life. "[Maternal eroticism is a] capacity to accompany the living, through the threat of mortality and even death" (Kristeva, 2014a, p. 78).[10]

This transformation of destruction, *the resignification of the abject*, is the revitalizing activity of reliance or maternal eroticism. In Kristeva's words,

In order for psychization to be finalized, and for biopsychical negativity to ensure the creation of links, maternal eroticism lets the death drive loose in the vital process, all while binding (*reliant*) the two together: the maternal transforms the abject (which the death drive has re-jected into the not-yet space of mother-child) into objects of care, into survival, and into life.

(2014a, p. 76)

Winnicott's conceptions of the holding function of the analyst, survival of destruction in transitional space (1960, 1971) as well as the positive pole of Green's (1986, 1999) 'work of the negative' reference such containing functions of the analyst. Extending the visual-spatial metaphor, these usable spaces might be viewed as *creating an envelope around which signifiers of the abject can emerge and are held*, becoming available for analytic work. As signifiers of the abject are re-transcribed through the love and care of the analyst's vitalizing interventions, signifiers of the abject become endowed with vitalizing features. These, then, can become objects of play, having been transformed into transitional objects (further explicated below).

PETRA: From abject signifiers to maternality

In our first telephone call when Petra requested analysis, she let me know that she did not want to look at me, *ever*. Indeed, she entered each session gaze averted and rushed to the couch, so as to quickly turn away. As she would lie there, she placed her hands over her eyes and face. She did not want to see me age, she explained. Consciously, her fear of my aging was related to the terrible deterioration of her mother when Petra was 22 years old. She watched her mother suffer with a blood disorder that eventually involved cognitive dementia. Her mother's blood was the site of her disease, coursing through her body, her platelets in short supply, failing to nurture her brain.

Petra chose to lie on the couch immediately, turning away as her hands remained covering her face. Her posture reminded me that some patients can use the couch to hide rather than reveal (Celenza, 2005). Petra had spent the last years of her mother's life in close proximity with her, ministering to her as she coped with a gradually encroaching dementia. By the time she started treatment with me, Petra had researched her *maternal female* relatives and found a preponderance of brain-related diseases, many of whom died at a young age. (Male transgenerational transmitters of such disease did not cross her mind.) Though she surrounded herself with these female biological facts of her family tree, she consciously tried to keep them out of her awareness. I did not realize until much later in the analysis that seeing me age carried with it a fear not only that I would become demented (and unable to hold her in mind) but that *she would be the contaminant who gave the germ to me.* Feelings of closeness through the treatment process seemed to trigger these obsessive worries. Would her germs *penetrate* me? Was *seeing* me dangerous to Petra? Was my *receptivity* to Petra dangerous to me? *Looking, gazing upon,* and *seeing* immediately conveyed powerful channels to project damage and in this way, were dangerous, contaminated, and contaminating modes of connection, as the transmission of germs seemed to go both ways.

Petra is a psychiatric nurse, married and at the time of beginning treatment, in her early 30s. She and her husband had begun talking about having children prompting Petra to enter treatment when she began to experience significant anxiety, almost to the point of panic. She assumed this had something to do with impending motherhood, but could not say how or in what way. She had always thought she wanted children.

Petra grew up in a middle-class home where her family lived well beyond their means, oriented toward presenting a wealthy appearance to the outside world. This required a frugal life style in the home, so that money was spent primarily in ways that would be ostentatiously displayed to others. Unsurprisingly, Petra requested a reduced fee from me which I knew was the beginning of an enacted scenario related in some way to her childhood experience with money. I agreed to a modest reduction to meet her halfway. This is how we began our work, the beginning of what I hoped would be a 4 times per week analysis. This came to be after months of gradually increasing sessions, as she found separations from me and the analysis more and more difficult. This occurred despite Petra's inability to verbally acknowledge a growing attachment between us.

Petra told me she had few female friends. She had experienced eroticized relationships with both male and female teachers – the erotic longings for a beloved female teacher confused her and raised questions in her mind about her sexual orientation. Erotic longings toward men further complicated these worries. At the beginning of our treatment, Petra told me she was uncertain about being in analysis with me because she "wasn't sure she could trust me." She linked this to my being a woman and added, "There's something about women." Sensing an important area for exploration, my queries did not yield further fantasies or feelings at this initial stage. Though I suspected important links between this ambiguous statement, the absence of female friends and fantasies linked with her early experience with her mother, she was unable to offer much beyond an idealized picture of her mother (as wholly empathic) and puzzlement about her friendships. The specter of her erotic attachments to female teachers also loomed large in the background of my mind. Within this early phase of the maternal transference, I also did not know if Petra's mistrust was linked to me as biologically, anatomically female or to my femininity (whatever this might mean to her).

In the early years of the analysis, Petra often brought up the issue of her reduced fee, stating a wish to pay my full fee. In the first year of our work, I adjusted and readjusted her fee – she would pay my full rate for a period of time, then she reversed this for another period of time. I viewed whatever enactment might be occurring surrounding the fee as a playspace to learn more about Petra's experience of my needs and her impact on me. The reduced fee caused her to fear that she was draining me of my resources, depleting my strength, and she feared I would become ill.

The maternal erotic transference in Petra

Maternal figures, through various maternal transferences, tend to arouse intense, early anxieties associated with desire along with a passivity and helplessness in relation to an all-powerful, enviable other (Chasseguet-Smirgel, 1976) and/or unconscious associations with the abject (Kristeva, 1980, 2014a, b). Unresolved mourning, derived from traumatic disappointments and/or loss of the mother, can indicate faulty internalizations of the maternal figure. Resting in the psyche as pathological introjects, these indicate the internalizing attempts to cope with traumatic loss in real life. These can be circumscribed and erupt in specific symptomatology in an otherwise high-functioning individual (as in the case of Petra) or become pervasive, with a more generalized impairment in functioning (see Perelberg, 2018).

Introjections or incorporations are types of internal psychic presences that exert an influence on the body and mind in an undigested, raw manner in order to preserve the object and then, may be experienced as a living thing inside. This inner presence can attack from within, from the inside out, as it were. Varying in quality and meaning, these introjects represent ego-dystonic or unassimilated part-objects (introjects) that have been internalized from traumatic experiences, often with the maternal figure. In some cases, introjects may become associated with signifiers of the abject. This is a good example of the ways in which female *qua female* (i.e., the mother as *anatomically* female, her *sexed* body) can become a site of de-vitalizing, pathological fears and horrors, where unconscious signifiers of the abject may emerge, thereby becoming accessible to analytic work.

As Kristeva (1980) states, "[The abject] is experienced at the peak of its strength when that subject ... finds the impossible within ... constitutes its very *being*, that it *is* none other than abject" (p. 5, italics in original). For Petra, the unconscious fantasy of her mother as a living (and potentially destructive) presence inside took the form of an illusory genetic predisposition to her mother's blood disease. Her intense anxiety led to a concretization in the form of fears of Petra's own decline and potential destructiveness to me (and presumably her anticipated unborn child). On a conscious level, Petra described her mother in largely idealized ways, as empathic, attuned, and loving. The absence of female friends stood in stark contrast as did her conflicts with me. At this time, she directly expressed intense mistrust, especially as hostile fantasies of my motives (e.g., surrounding my fee) surfaced and she directly associated these fantasies with my being a woman. This transference played out in the up and down negotiations around my fee, which we soon discovered revolved around an alternating sadomasochistic dynamic: a reduced fee resulted in fantasies of my imminent demise unconsciously caused by her depleting me and, alternatively, fantasies of her *own* depletion caused by *me* during times when she paid my full fee. The latter can be seen in the following:

P: You must feel I'm an easy target for you. I need you, I'm so anxious, you know it and you know so much about me now. I'm trapped in this process, trapped with you! I even sometimes think that you'll make me stay forever ... trapping me and not wanting me to leave for *your* financial gain. But what good does it do *me*, anyway?

A: You worry you'll be trapped in a bottomless pit, that *I* have trapped you with my greed and selfishness. All for me, nothing for you.

P: I'm afraid to tell you about things I've spent money on, clothes I buy, where I go on vacation. Like you'd object and be furious that I'm spending money when I don't always pay your full fee.

But now I am! And I can't stand it! I think you're greedy and want to take anything I might have. How am I supposed to get better, anyway?

A: You fear there's something inside, you or me, that could destroy us both.

P: We can't both be losing in this bargain. I know I sound so money-obsessed, but it's this thing about you being a woman. A taker. Devious. Yet I know this isn't true.

During these early months, Petra could not express these desires directly to me and her reversals were fiercely held, leading her to believe that she hated me. The intensity of these convictions exposed the passion fueling her fears and she worried if she should stay in the analysis with such a greedy, exploitative, and manipulative person. It was during this time that Petra reported occasional masturbatory fantasies where I punished her for the pleasure she was experiencing.

Unsurprisingly, Petra wondered whether the analysis was going to help her, since she thought her intense doubts about my trustworthiness and 'bottomless self-interest' were bad signs. Yet, she never missed a session and found the weekends increasingly difficult to tolerate. I told her I understood how she was experiencing her fears, but that I viewed *her ability to tell me* about her feelings, however intense and negative, paradoxically demonstrated her trust in me and her ability to use the analysis. In my countertransference, I could feel her growing attachment and her fiercely held negations, the looking away, and fearful aspects of her countenance only affirmed (for me) how important I was becoming to her.

Unbeknownst to me at this time, Petra was wearing a special sweater as she lay on the couch, in order to allow the sweater to *touch* the upholstery of the couch. She would then bring the sweater home, sleep with it under her pillow, and carry it with her during the day. She eventually told me about this secretive, concretized *taking me in*, and explained that she did this so that she could feel comforted between sessions. She told me she was consistently doing this, unable to wash the sweater for fear of washing off my scent and presence. I asked her if she wanted to take something of mine from the office, to have something symbolic of our work together and representative of our relationship. She was surprised by my reaction, wondering why I wasn't put off, insulted, or even repulsed by her. She said, "Oh come on! On a scale from 1-10, you have to tell me how pathological this is!" When I responded with an emphatic "Zero!" she *looked at me* seemingly for the first time. She took an item off my bookshelf and placed it in her purse, arguably enacting an erotic move of containing me by placing the precious object in her 'purse,' seemingly solidifying the erotic nature of this exchange.

The work of the negative and the abject in Petra

In these early years of analysis, for Petra, *touching* me (in displacement, through various transitional objects) and *seeing* me were sites of both conflict and potential resolution. Petra spoke of contamination – does she make her *patients* sick, will her patients make *her* sick, and she worried about making *me* sick. Germs were a regular character in the field (Ferro, 1999) and she was alert to my voice sounding congested, if I sneezed or coughed, if I was late or, worst of all, if I forgot something.

There are many related conceptualizations in the literature that speak to the subjective experience of emptiness, a sense of void or hauntedness, as our analysands report chronic feelings of dread or doom. This sense of dread or emptiness can complicate experiences of *taking in* elements of the outside world as the sense of danger is externalized. Petra describes her fears of contamination as an indescribable, yet chronic pit in her stomach, like an empty space that threatens to overtake her, culminating in fears that receptivity to others would expose her to contamination or that she will contaminate others. She worried if she would give this sense of dread to me. At times, I imagined Petra poised at the edge of an abyss into which she feared I had already fallen and that I was hiding this fact from her.

When is an abyss a threatening void and how to transform this void within the usable (potential) space of analysis? The abyss or dreaded void that Petra describes is aligned with Green's (1986) *work of the negative*, reflective of traumatic foreclosures that deny separation and loss. The empty void in the child's phenomenal subjective experience threatens the child with intolerable loss, unresolvable enigmas, and confusions; it is the unthought known (Bollas, 1989) like a dread or haunting. It is preoedipal, nonverbal, and unbounded, harboring ghosts that echo annihilatory chants. Kristeva's (1980, 2014a, b) abject lies here, perhaps in disowned fragments, subliminal, or unrepresented.

As noted, Petra wanted yet felt guilty about her reduced fee. She raised the subject frequently, offering to pay more which she then did for a period of time, only to request a reduction again in a few months. She feared draining me, depleting my strength, and making me ill. I suggested to her that pennies and platelets are precious objects that need to be tracked and saved. We surmised that cents (c-e-n-t-s) and sense (s-e-n-s-e) were the poetry of her unconscious.

The enacted play surrounding the fee provided a forum to realize meaningful props in Petra's unconscious. These took the form of precious yet phobically avoided part-objects (e.g., germs, money, dying platelets), signifiers of the abject (Kristeva, 1980, 2014a, b), heretofore meaningless, awesome, and horrifying things in the process of acquiring significance. I see Petra's focus on germs, money, and blood as representing her anxieties about death and destructiveness, constructed through the work of the death drive (devitalization through the abject) and the work of the negative (Green, 1999), all linked to fears of her capacity to harm (me, her patients, her family). Pennies and platelets seemed to be symbolized displacements to an arena where the concretized *signifiers of the abject*, i.e., introjected part-objects of destruction, became (in fantasy) capable of being tamed, controlled, and possessed – also acquiring a sense of permanence. I suggest that these concretizations, around which Petra obsessively worried, reflected the presence of pathological *signifiers of the abject* that lived in the abyss of her unconscious, as if (metaphorically) in foreclosed spaces swirling in an implosive black hole. In Petra's case, the germs, blood, and dying platelets (associated in her mind with being anatomically female) represented signifiers of the abject, introjected and feared as potential contaminants to herself and others.

Throughout the treatment with Petra, I offered her a type of containment that directly countered her pathological introjects. For example, I never retaliated, my sturdiness remained steadfast, nor did I psychically disappear or become paralyzed when she spoke of my greediness and her hatred of me. She would now say, "I'm dumbfounded that you let me say these things and you don't get defensive! I feel so grateful, but now I feel guilty too ...." Each time I welcomed her things, touched them, let her things touch my body, and survived, I detoxified the germs, as if to convey that my maternal reliance was stronger than her feared germs and blood. This led to an increasing ability to open herself emotionally to me, herself, and others.

Back to Petra

In the first years of the analysis, Petra talked about her early childhood as surrounded by her mother's presence and care, physically affection-ate and empathic to her emotional well-being. This idealized picture was linked to memories of sitting on her mother's lap, hugs abounding with lots of touching. This directly contrasted with Petra's manner of relating to me where she seemed unwilling, unable, or afraid to look at me or *take me in* in other ways. I did not know if the placement of her hands over her face was designed to prevent her from seeing me (as she had said) or to prevent *me* from seeing *her*.

Zeavin (2019) makes a useful distinction between an internal good mother and an internal idealized mother, the latter implying an active, unconscious need to keep her mother good, evidence that something bad threatens to mar the maternal imago. Such an internalized dynamic was indicated by Petra's anxious attentiveness to my well-being, her attempts to reassure herself that she had not harmed me, and that I was unblemished and would not harm her.

Later in the analysis, a shift occurred in Petra's internal world as she relayed an incident when she was 12 years old where she had wit-nessed a physical fight between her brother and a neighbor. Petra's mother had allowed the neighbor to enter their home whereupon he began to taunt her brother, a teasing which ended in a serious physi-cal altercation. When her brother was badly beaten and rendered help-less, the neighbor left of his own accord. Petra's mother and herself stood by, paralyzed, and in shock. The neighbor was never confronted nor did Petra's mother tell her father or the police. Worse, her mother implied that Petra may have been the reason the neighbor wanted to visit, a comment that implied something about Petra's sexuality. She remained confused by this insinuation and never understood why her mother failed to report the incident to either her father or the police. This was not a new memory, but in the *après coup* of the analytic process, the memory now reflected a re-transcription of linked images of her mother. This re-transcription unmasked the idealized maternal introjects and elaborated her memories of her mother as sometimes *not* present, even failing her, and capable of persecuting her.

It was during this time that my own mother became ill, a long pro-cess of decline after which she eventually died. Cancerous tumors had broken through her skin and, at times, would bleed profusely. I minis-tered to her, mingling my being with her blood, cleaning her up, reas-suring her that she did not smell, and comforting her with surrounding, tearful embraces in these last months of her life. We achieved an emotional union that we never had before.

When I returned to our sessions, Petra brought in some objects that she wanted me to hold for a few minutes, transmitting (in her mind) my psychically soothing capacities to the objects she had brought, soon to be transformed and capable of soothing her. I did not hesitate to hold these objects (a stone and a small wooden box), holding them firmly between my hands. Then she brought out a shawl, sheepishly offering it to me to do the same with it. I immediately took the shawl and placed it around my shoulders. I left it there for about 20 seconds. Petra was stunned that I would so easily "let her things touch me" and she watched me welcome her presence, through the shawl and my body, as our beings intermingled. I believe this was not simply 'putting on a shawl' and the various holding functions that act might symbolize. This was a moment when Petra experienced me *willing to risk death*, and more particularly, to risk closeness with her destructiveness and murderous capabilities.

Around this time, Petra was able to address ways in which her mother was physically present but psychically absent and even bad (paralyzed, submissive, and potentially persecutory). She expressed her gratitude that I would be "so kind and patient with my crazy," referring to her various fears, hateful sentiments, and the use of transitional objects to have me endow them with soothing capacities.

I believe I was able to offer Petra this intimate touching (and its fantastical psychic soothing) *without hesitation* due to the experiences with my mother and all the touching, seeing, and holding that had entailed. I further believe this message was unconsciously transmitted to Petra in a way that made the containment of her longings to *see* and *touch me*, (i.e., to *take me in*), detoxified and uncontaminated. In talking about these experiences and the meanings they had for her, Petra spoke of experiencing me as unafraid, sturdy, and "openly willing to accept her crazy needs." She talked about the smell of her sweater after being in my office and I was reminded of my experience with my mother, especially the fact that she had directly asked me if she smelled, apparently worried about the blood from her tumors on her body. Felicitously, Petra and I added s-c-e-n-t-s (to 'cents' and 'sense') to the collection of concretizations representing Petra's precious objects, now as healthy identifications, having been transformed through a re-vitalization of signifiers of the abject.

My conjecture is that changes in me (through the parallel process of my own mother dying while remarkably and for the first time, coming alive to me), enlarged my receptivity to Petra's re-transcription of her own memories of her mother. I was not afraid of touching my mother, the moments of fluid exchange – blood, tears, and love. These were not abstract experiences, but highly personal, passionate, and embodied, what Wilson (2014) artfully names "that place of the flesh" (p. 103). My memories of this experience with my mother were directly translated into a capacity to offer the same to Petra.

From inhibited passivity to disciplined receptivity

In the psychic envelope of the analyst's containing function, signifiers of the abject can emerge and become available to the analytic process. For Petra, the crux of this work revolved around differentiating her mother's traumatizing passivity and paralysis from my disciplined and enduring receptivity that invited her into the usable space of analytic process. I suggest such disciplined receptivity can be viewed as an *eternal signifier of the maternal*, clearly a part of Kristeva's (2014a, b) vitalizing and re-vitalizing components of reliance.

In this way, Petra's worry about contaminating me can be viewed as an *erotically* tinged anxiety related to all manner of vitalizing 'taking in.' Longing for identification had brought with it a fear that she would contaminate and ultimately harm me. Seeing, touching, and knowing me were all forbidden as the witnessing of the assault on her brother had contaminated her and, connected to that experience, the traumatically disappointing maternal response.

In the months following Petra's gradual de-idealization of her mother, she reported to me that she no longer worried about my frailty nor that she would harm me in some way. I also noticed she no longer hid behind her hands while lying on the couch. Soon there ushered in a hypersensitivity with me in relation to her and anything she might say. She said, "The more precious you are to me, the more scared I am of losing you. It's the depth, it feels like soul to soul. I get greedy for it. I want to feel it all the time." These sentiments intensified and characterized the next phase of analytic work. On another occasion, she said, "It's like romantic feelings – I worry about every little thing, like I'm going to do something wrong and you'll break up with me!" These changes coincided with an ability to directly look at me as well as masturbatory fantasies that no longer involved me punishing her, but as inviting her pleasure in her body. I experienced these changes as demonstrative of her ability to *take me in* as part of her subjective experience in the analysis. It was also around this time that she and her husband began trying to have a child.

Notes

1 I also believe it is useful to imagine a multiplicity of selves on racial, ethno-cultural, socioeconomic, and age-related levels, but these are not the subject of the present discussion (see Celenza, 2010).
2 Though the sexed and gendered psychic fantasies of the pregnant mother about the baby begin in utero and are unconsciously transmitted to the baby from birth onward, these will be translated by the baby through various unconscious mechanisms after birth.
3 (1989, p. 133, quoted in Perelberg [2018]).
4 In the following discussion of maternal eroticism, I will use the pronouns she and her despite the awareness that the primary caregiver is not necessarily a woman. Despite the variability in anatomical sex of the primary caregiver, however, it is my contention that maternal eroticism is a playground within which the child comes to unconsciously represent femaleness and femininity, necessarily co-opting available linguistic categories from the socio-cultural surround.
5 I have selected the term *signifier* to connote *carrier of (conscious or unconscious) meaning*. I do not use the term in the context of Lacanian theorizing, but prefer the term *signifier* to symbol, imago, representation, and various types of internalization because signifier is general in its connotation and does not specify a form (i.e., verbal, nonverbal, imagistic, sensory) or mode of internalization.
6 The term abject literally means the state of being utterly hopeless, miserable, humiliated, or wretched (https://www.dictionary.com/browse/abject?s=t).
7 See Celenza (2014) for a discussion of sexual dysfunction related to unconscious fears of the maternal vagina.
8 Wilson (2014) discusses the dream of Irma's injection where Freud examines her throat and is horrified upon seeing a "big white patch" and "whitish gray scabs." He recognizes this experience as Freud's encounter with the *real* (in Lacanian terms) and Kristeva's theorizing of the "unnameable, prior, fleshy, feminine place," encompassed by maternal reliance (p. 105).
9 A concordance in theorizing that Kristeva herself notes: "Overflowing its bounds … by the labor of abjection … reliance is clearly the work of the negative" (Kristeva, 2014a, p. 77).
10 Wilson (2014) expands on this maternal responsibility, what Kristeva (2014a) felicitously terms "*her*ethics" (p. 82, emphasis on 'her') and incisively describes maternal containment as "a willingness to wonder, an expectation to engage, and the transformation of hate into an embodied sense of caring that enacts 'knowledge' of life and death and the fragility of the entire arrangement" (Wilson, 2014, p. 107). In these ways, the re-vitalizing components of maternal eroticism, especially in its commitment and responsibility toward (*re*)-vitalization and holding of aggressive impulses (Winnicott, 1971), parallels the analytic purpose and process.

Chapter 6

Comfort and containment of erotic language and feelings

In this chapter, I wrestle with the question of the analyst's comfort with erotic language and a directly related concern, the verbal disclosure of erotic countertransference.[1] The ability to contain feelings aroused in both erotic transferences and countertransferences will depend on the analyst's comfort in the overall terrain and will directly affect dilemmas surrounding technique, especially those of self-disclosure. Is the analyst's disclosure of erotic feelings toward her/his analysand ever clinically indicated? How far can we allow our participation and emotional engagement with the patient to be explicitly articulated? And most importantly, under what conditions might the disclosure of erotic countertransference be permissible and even warranted?

The need for this chapter is prompted by my work consulting on the problem of sexual boundary transgressions, but also my awareness (from supervisory settings, academic contexts, and other professional contexts) that analysts and psychoanalytically-oriented therapists do verbalize their loving and/or erotic feelings more than is formally reported. This clinical reality needs to be brought under the umbrella of transparent clinical discourse so that the questions and conundrums attendant to these moments can be examined and discussed.

Further, my appreciation for the need to discuss self-disclosure of erotic feelings is also prompted by debates on these challenges, mostly within the relational literature. I firmly believe it is not enough to have a mandate that clinicians refrain from directly expressing any or all modes of feeling. Clinicians do not abide by this and are not helped by such a blanket prohibition. It is also questionable whether our patients are helped by such blanket restraint. Despite Shakespeare's admonition to "learn to read what silent love hath writ,"[2] the verbal acknowledgment of loving feelings can touch, in a more concrete way, the longings

DOI: 10.4324/9781003391012-6

and vulnerabilities our patients seek to heal. On the other hand, such acknowledgments can also seduce our patients and/or deepen dependencies and expectations to find with us that which they need to nurture and cultivate within themselves and in their external lives. Such are the conundrums about which this chapter wrestles.

There are now a few (counted on one hand) examples in the clinical literature on the explicit revelation of erotic countertransference, beginning with Jody Davies' (1994) paper, "Love in the Afternoon: A Relational Reconsideration of Desire and Dread in the Countertransference," where she revealed a courageous and controversial disclosure that she had made to her patient. Davies told him that she "has had sexual fantasies about [him], many times" (p. 166).[3] In response to much of the debate that her paper generated, Davies (1998b) observed a phobic dread of erotic transference and countertransference due to the absence of theory. To this, I add the absence of clear guidelines for technique and this chapter is an attempt to address this gap.

Almost immediately after publication, Davies' (1994) paper instigated a torrent of authors weighing in on the use and misuse of disclosure of erotic countertransference with most advising against it except in unusual circumstances. Gabbard (1994) warned of unduly burdening the patient and foreclosing mourning. Benjamin (1994b) wondered about the role of power and hate in the interaction. Cooper (1998) advised "virtual disclosure," a statement that implies the analyst is willing to explore the patient's perceptions [of the analyst as a desiring other] while not definitively affirming the analyst's perspective. Both Gabbard (1994, 1996) and Benjamin (1997) emphasized the role of the analyst in protecting transitionality. Gabbard also cites Modell's (1991) writings that the asymmetry in the analytic setting is not an asymmetry of desire but an asymmetry of *the communication* of desire. Mann (1994) argues that erotic countertransference disclosure would only serve to stimulate incestuous wishes. Cornell (2008) believes direct disclosure of the analyst's personal, sexual interest, or disinterest trivializes the erotic space. Hirsch (1994) directs us to the relational-conflict model of psychoanalytic theory for guidance in making use of the analyst's private countertransference feelings.

On the other side are those analysts who argue that judicious and tactful disclosure of erotic countertransference can facilitate the treatment (see Lijtmaer, 2004, for a helpful review). Knoblauch (1995) observes other affects that often go unexplored and unarticulated due to 'something else that occurred' in the moment of erotic disclosure, such as anxiety and fear of the analyst's actions. Slavin et al. (1998) believe erotic countertransference disclosures can facilitate the demystification of infantile conflicts. Hoffman (2009) suggests that, while no single standardized mode of expression is generalizable, the "challenge for each of us is ... to express that passionate response in a manner that is usable by each patient" (p. 635).

A more recent example is, ironically, embedded in a paper written as a celebratory discussion of Davies' (1994) paper 20 years later, by Jill Gentile (2013), entitled, "From *Truth or Dare* to *Show and Tell*: Reflections on Childhood Ritual, Play and the Evolution of Symbolic Life." In this discussion, Gentile describes a moment in her treatment of a patient, Mr. G, where she holds his beloved wooden baseball bat from childhood, offered to her during a session. Gentile's musings at the time included her awareness of multiple symbolic meanings for the patient, including the phallic imagery. At one point, she put the bat across her chair like a barrier and acknowledged to him that perhaps she is afraid she may get a little too excited for her comfort, if not for his, and for their work together. Despite the negation and future tense (i.e., "she may get" as opposed to "she is"), she presents Mr. G with the possibility of her embodied arousal. The use of physical objects (toys) had been frequent in the treatment with Mr. G and Gentile has a lovely way of likening the process to play therapy, defining the various dynamics in terms of structured games, including *Hide and Seek*, *Truth or Dare*, *Show and Tell* as well as *Lost and Found*. I have no problem with these analogies nor with the presentation of physical objects and their use, a common enough occurrence in many treatments, usually in the form of gifts. Most importantly, Gentile keeps her eye and analytic discipline intact by exploring the meanings of the various toys at every turn, including the implied erotic messages in many.

One factor that is important to note embedded in both Davies' (1994) and Gentile's (2013) vignettes is that both authors acknowledged *a context wherein some important therapeutic work needed to be accomplished.* For Davies, it was a final moment of impasse, during the termination phase of a successful treatment that had, nevertheless, left a crucial piece of work undone. For Gentile, the moment in the treatment that led to the disclosure revolved around the patient's experience of himself as a potent man, perhaps wanting to test and claim his prowess through offering various symbolic props to his analyst. The issue I am to highlight here is that the disclosures were made with the hope and intent (at least consciously) to perform some therapeutic piece of work. We might surmise that the analyst's countertransference experience was likely to be layered, with some measure of anxiety, confusion, and/or frustration, however these are not made explicit and we cannot definitively know. Necessity being the mother of invention, the rationale for the disclosure followed salutary lines, and in Davies' case, includes disclaimers that all other possible analytic responses had been tried and failed. In Gentile's case, the erotic countertransference disclosure seems to occur organically, as a moment in an otherwise playful, even flirtatious process aimed at expanding the symbolic play-space. Holding the bat created a "markedness" that served to hold the line between the concrete and the symbolic.[4] Perhaps the placement of the bat (across her lap) symbolized a similar marking and Gentile trusted her patient to interpret these markings without confusion or overstimulation. I do not doubt the descriptions of either process material and in the spirit of collaboration and furthering our thinking about these crucial therapeutic choice points, I offer the following thoughts.

The undisclaimable analytic frame

There is, from my point of view, a tendency to justify analyst self-disclosure, especially when the content is positive, affectionate, loving, or even erotic, by making reference to the *mutual* dimension of the analytic relationship and adducing (I think, mistakenly) that the disclosure is encompassed entirely from within this dimension. I believe understanding disclosures in this way overemphasizes the mutuality inherent in the analytic process while minimizing or even ignoring the equally persistent, continual, and simultaneous dimension of asymmetry.

Aside from the important need to be mindful of the context in which any disclosure is made, it is imperative to keep in mind that the very dimensions that define the analytic frame (those of *mutuality and asymmetry*) also intensify the patient's experience and longing for intimate, sexual union in this context.[5] All of the structural dimensions of the analytic set-up define the boundaries of the process and cannot be disclaimed, i.e., when we accept payment for services, we symbolically accept responsibility to maintain the various power imbalances while mutually participating in the endeavor.

A related issue to erotic countertransference disclosure that is often raised as a rationale in favor of disclosure, especially in cases of sexual boundary transgressions, is the extent to which the patient may be viewed as a responsible adult and the corollary issue, how the analyst should take responsibility for her/his participation. How one views the assumptions inferred in these questions will bear on the technical decisions and their rationales regarding erotic countertransference disclosure. Hoffman (2009) asserts that the patient is a separate person with a will and is "not putty in the analyst's hands" with the capacity to agree, differ, and collaborate in meaningful ways (p. 619). I do not disagree with this assertion, however I believe the quality and extent of psychological autonomy and self-control, even separateness, for all of the above-named capacities fluctuates during the course of treatment and, especially under the sway of an intense erotic transference, can be reduced to nil for a protracted period of time. In addition, it is important to remember that the patient (and analyst) are not only adults to each other, but in a multiplicity of self-states wherein any one or many may be in the foreground or background at a particular point in time. There is a child within the adult as well as the wish to be potential lovers, even when these modes of relating are not in the immediate, conscious, or foregrounded experience.

Further, I suggest that the development of an erotic transference and the capacity to be under its spell for a period of time is a strength, a capacity to be fully receptive to the analytic process and the intensity of affects it evokes. This capacity to give oneself over to the process in a more or less complete way is parallel to the classical notion of a transference neurosis, once believed to be a *sine qua non* of analyzability. Therefore, I do not intend to imply that the patient is any less of an adult under the sway of an intense erotic transference but rather, has cultivated the capacity to become fully receptive to a set of emotional reactions that she/he may not have control over for a period of time.

Because the analytic process is mutual and because we participate in it, we have varying stakes in what we want or need at any one time. This means there is the possibility of defensively disclaiming one aspect or another of this complex interchange and our capacity for self-deception should never be underestimated, even for the highly sophisticated theoretician and experienced, seasoned analyst. For example, we can exclusively focus on our own personal meanings or intentions while denying the patients. Often I have heard, "That phrase was not erotic, I had no intention of crossing that line," or, "I am very clear on the boundaries … I told her I loved her and I meant it in a Platonic way." In these statements, the analyst selectively disattends to the patient's experience or fantasies, including how she or he might attribute a different meaning to the very same words. It is not enough to be clear about one's own intent and there is a responsibility to refrain from engaging in actions that might be misconstrued. When we focus on the patient's experience, we engage our capacity to appreciate and monitor the asymmetry in the analytic relationship.

Frequently, there is a minimization of the erotic potential in otherwise seemingly non-erotic language. We may desexualize, in the moment, words that at some later point may represent a highly charged conveyance. Language itself is elastic; surface and depth easily overlap manifest and latent meanings. More importantly, the treatment setting is rife with sexual metaphor – as noted in earlier chapters, the penetrating gaze and interpretative activity of the analyst can be experienced as 'coming inside.' Similarly, the background all-enveloping support of the analyst's affirmative attitude and concrete office (including the couch itself) can engender feelings of sensual erotic longings.[6]

Comfort and clarity with erotic language

Especially for those patients whose presenting areas of distress involve sexual inhibitions, defensively eroticized activity, or compulsions, the analytic setting will provide ample opportunity to demonstrate erotic longings in metaphorized, displaced, and hopefully directly expressed modes. Conversely, sexualized material presented as pervasive or intensely preoccupying may be revealed as masking non-erotic longings. In any case, attunement to sexual metaphor and comfort with erotic language will be essential in aiding a patient's self-understanding and the ability to explore her/his erotic life.

This reminds me of an episode that occurred during my own analysis. I'd had an erotic dream about my analyst and when I awoke, I thought to myself, "Cool!" As far as I knew, I wanted this to happen and I looked forward to telling my analyst all about it. So I got in my car and began the drive to his office, as had become automatic, having driven there 4 times a week for three years. It's fair to say, I knew the way. On this particular morning, the 563rd time – (I did the math, including Bunker Hill Day and Flag Day, which my analyst considered "scam holidays" – but I digress), I inexplicably and for the first time in 3 years, missed the exit to Brookline off Storrow Drive. Further, I did not notice that I was on my way downtown Boston until I arrived at none other than 'Government Center' … Superego City.

By the time I retraced my steps, chuckling all the while yet also realizing I was more uncomfortable than I could admit, I finally arrived at my analyst's office with just enough time remaining to explain what had happened. No time to tell the dream on that day. Apparently, in its efforts to derail, my unconscious kept track of the time. When I left his office, my analyst said, "See you tomorrow ... maybe." We may think we are more comfortable than we actually are.

For many patients, the language of the treatment becomes more direct, shame-free, and thereby more intimate as the treatment progresses. This does not imply the need or therapeutic value of disclosing the analyst's erotic feelings for the patient, however, though it may be more tempting to do so with greater comfort in the discourse. I am emphasizing here a comfort with erotic language that is used to explicate and directly clarify *the patient's longings and experience*, on conscious and unconscious levels, as they arise in either disguised or direct forms. Hoffman (2009) asks, "Why, in fact, do we favor implicit over explicit forms of affirmation, indeed, implicit over explicit expressions of love?" My response is simple: we always favor explicit forms of expressions of affirmation and love, including erotic longings *from the patient's point of view, but not from the analyst's* because love is a four-letter word.

At the same time, the appreciation of the stimulating potential of direct expressions of the analyst's erotic longing or love must always be balanced with the need to be comfortable, explicit, and non-euphemistic in expressing erotic themes. Galit Atlas (2016) recounts a moment in a treatment with a female patient where the analyst repeated, exactly the way her patient had expressed it, an erotic phrase about a man she had been dating:

"In the dream you give him a blowjob," [Atlas says]. Ella giggles, "Oh no, it sounds terrible coming out of your mouth." [Atlas] get[s] confused for a moment and wonder[s] whether this was not the term that Ella had used. "Did I phrase it differently?" [Atlas asks]. "No, not at all," Ella replies, "That's exactly what I said, it's just so strange to hear it... it's easier to say it... maybe even easier to do it," she jokes...

(pp. 17–18)

The analyst should speak about sex in plain language, as Atlas demonstrates, especially in ways the patient is familiar and the process should proceed to expand the discourse in this direction. I mention this vignette here, however, to highlight how powerful and saturated with meaning our words are to our patients. When *we* say something, it is not the same as when our *patient's do*.[7] It is not symmetrical nor is it predictable, but at the same time, we need to cultivate a measure of ease in speaking about sexuality and erotic life. One way to 'break the ice' in cultivating ease is to do what Atlas did, to repeat our patient's words exactly as they express their desires in order to facilitate a mutual comfort and hopefully advance the discourse as the work proceeds. But again, this is always from the perspective of the patient's point of view.

One supervisee was uncomfortable repeating her male patient's desire to be "fucked up the ass" (his words) yet knew she had to refer to his erotic desires in some way in order to explore them. I suggested to her that she repeatedly say the phrase out loud in her car (windows closed) to acquire more comfort with his way of putting it. She did this and became more comfortable using his phrase in their work.

The delicate balance that I aim to put forth, *ease with erotic discourse while maintaining the focus on the patient's desires* is illustrated in another clinical vignette. A patient was in the midst of an intense erotic transference for many months. He was explicitly fixated on the need to know if I was erotically attracted to him. He stated that he did not care whether I liked him or even loved him, but wanted to know what my sexual feelings were for him. This quality of the transference arose in the context of his uncertainty of his desirability toward women in general and whether they wanted to have sex with him. Questions about his potency and doubts about his 'masculine' attributes were lifelong struggles and had a severely inhibiting effect on his ability to perform sexually.

At this particular time in the treatment, this patient and I were in the midst of a heated transference/countertransference dance where his longings and my desires were relatively in sync and I had hoped my attraction to him would be palpably apparent to him. To be simple and direct, I was aware of being sexually attracted to him and hoped he could feel this though I had not directly articulated my feelings to him nor did I intend to do so. He consistently stated that he was unsure how I felt about him and that he needed to know, at times he insisted he would be cured if I would only say yea or nay to this crucial question. (Believe me, it was tempting.)

One day, this patient came to our session and offered me a gift, a rectangular box covered with beautiful Asian silk. Inside were two Chinese Health Balls. (I think these used to be called *Worry Balls* and yes, they were about the size of two testicles.) He asked me to take them out of the box and gestured how they are held "in order to release stress." I couldn't help but chuckle a bit and I probably also blushed, but what I said was, "You want me to see and feel your potency … to touch your balls." Before the reader cringes with embarrassment and dismisses this interchange as one that could not possibly be uttered with either seriousness or therapeutic intent, I must add that this patient and I had cultivated a way of speaking about his sexual desires, his body, and his sexual functioning that by now was an organic part of our discourse. This was the 4th year of a moving analysis and I knew I could speak to him using such blunt language. (This is not particularly unique to this patient and me; I try to cultivate similar plain speak with all of my patients, especially those with sexual symptoms or inhibitions. Not all patients develop an ease with such language, but I do see the development of some measure of comfort as part of the analytic work.)

At the time of this vignette and after I had expressed the above statement, this patient seemed immediately struck, not by my language, but by how he had unconsciously displayed his desires. Because he had already directly, in words, expressed these desires to me, he was not shocked or ashamed by the unconscious meaning of his gift. He also was able to experience some pleasure in my interpretation of the possible unconscious meaning, chuckling at the stark simplicity and almost innocence of his conscious intent. It was a moment of truth (Slavin, 2013) that acknowledged in words what we each already knew he felt. Ultimately, we were both amused by his unconscious selection.

Verbal disclosure of erotic countertransference

In all of the vignettes I have read involving a disclosure of erotic countertransference, I am always left with a lingering question. Why didn't the analyst maintain her/his focus on the patient's experience rather than respond to the patient's expressed wish (at least on the surface) to be told what the analyst feels toward her/him? It is my experience that the wish to *know the analyst sexually* is invariably complicated and usually highly conflicted. And if it is not, *it should be*, given the inherent power imbalances and (oedipal) transference structure from where the desire likely arises. Herein lies another responsibility of the analyst – to explicate the various levels of meaning in the patient's erotic desire for the analyst as someone who is virtually or at least explicitly unknown.

I realize all of our patients have a sense of our being, personality, and style; I do not engage nor endorse some impossible objectivist striving toward anonymity. But the analytic contract involves the conscious asymmetric distribution of attention and focus to remain on the patient's experience, so why is there a push, in some extraordinary moments, to shine the spotlight on the analyst's experience? I also realize we use our awareness of our feelingful engagement at all times to receive unconscious communications and to inform our affective responses to the patient, but the responsive focus remains on the patient's experience, even if we explicitly verbalize some of the ways in which we have metabolized, processed, or experienced the patient (see Renik, 1999).

Despite the unusual power distributions and uneven focus of attention in the analytic relationship, it is still a human interaction with ongoing mutual, bi-directional passionate engagement. In addition, our patients come to us for help with affect regulation and desires for transformation by advancing their understanding of their emotional and erotic desires. Emotional constriction in the analyst would hardly help in this enterprise. However, too often the defensive uses of erotic feelings can mask corrupting influences in the treatment and our capacity for self-deception must always sound a cautionary note.

Necessary conditions of erotic countertransference disclosure

I will directly address the conditions under which verbal erotic countertransference disclosure may be permissible and perhaps even warranted by introducing an extended vignette and then offering explicit guidelines. The context for the way in which this verbal disclosure by the analyst came about was indirect and circuitous, but it is an example of an explicit, verbal disclosure of erotic countertransference that I believe meets the conditions for which such an intervention is permissible.

A supervisee was putting together a write-up to present a case at a clinical conference, a vignette, and corresponding discussion that contained a description, privately held by her, of her loving, affectionate, and erotic countertransference with a patient. In preparing for the conference, she had obtained the patient's consent to write about an interchange that had occurred during the late phase of a successful analysis and in writing about this interchange, she described her passionate, affectionate, and erotic feelings for him in preparation for the presentation. When he gave his permission for the presentation, she invited him to read what she would be presenting with the intention that she would redact the dicey parts about her own feelings toward him. Interestingly, he refused the invitation to read her write-up, getting her off the hook at least for the moment. He said, "I don't want to interrupt what's going on between us right now." She prepared the write-up and presented the case at the clinical conference.

A year later, during the termination phase of the treatment, the patient asked to read what she had written. With some mixture of curiosity and trepidation, she printed out the write-up, *purposefully unredacted*, and handed it to him. He read it then and there, during the session. As I mentioned, the write-up included a description of her erotic countertransference toward him. Though it was not detailed, she explicitly said that she returned the sexual attraction that he had felt toward her. Her acknowledgments in the write-up were embedded in descriptions of love and affection for him and appreciation of his various personality attributes.

As part of the background in this case, it should be mentioned that periodically during the treatment, this patient had expressed his longing and attraction toward his analyst. He was happily married and the treatment had solidified his bond with his wife as well. Though the analyst never explicitly told him she found him sexually attractive, she did sense that he knew how she felt, given how safe he felt he was with her and how obvious her enjoyment of him was. Several times, he stated directly that he thought he knew how she felt about him and understood she could not express her feelings directly. In short, he could *feel* their mutual attraction.[8]

After reading the write-up, which included at least two instances where she spelled out her affection for him, her enjoyment of his sense of humor, and her erotic attraction to him, he said, "I am so touched." He went on to say,

I already knew this was how you felt. In fact, I've told you how you feel about me many times! But it's nice to have it returned in an explicit way. I will keep this tucked away in my heart forever.

She teared up when he said this and there was a palpable mutual appreciation for each other.

You might think this vignette and my approval of the way my supervisee handled this interchange contradicts all I have discussed thus far about verbal disclosure of erotic countertransference (Table 6.1). To my mind, it does not for the following reasons, all of which are interrelated.

In relation to all of these conditions, I will now consider each in relation to the clinical/supervisory vignette presented above.

First, and most importantly, the patient already had surmised, sensed, thought about, and 'knew' his analyst returned his erotic feelings. How did he sense this? My supervisee is a passionate woman and does not withhold her *nonverbal responsivity* and passionate involvement in her relationships. That is different from explicitly revealing her feelings, putting them into words, and making them the focus in the session.[9]

Second, the treatment had helped this patient hone his antennae for detecting his impact on others, in particular strengthening his ability and confidence in his capacity to erotically arouse another person. Thus, he *did not need* a verbal confirmation and, most importantly, the revelation of the analyst's feelings was not necessary to effect these advances in the therapeutic action. His capacity to surmise her attraction to him is a strength that partially grew out of the treatment and her disclosure was not aimed to fill a gap in his capacity to detect this.

Table 6.1 Conditions for Disclosure of Erotic Countertransference

- The analysand already knows how the analyst feels
- The analysand has the capacity to "read what silent love hath writ" i.e., can accurately surmise the other's mental state and feelings
- It is the termination phase when therapeutic work is largely addressed; important mourning of relationship has occurred
- The analysand is high-functioning, unlikely to be confused or overstimulated
- The analyst is aware of risks and the performative nature of words
- The analyst is in consultation over these issues
- The analyst is contained in relation to personal needs and self-care

Third, the disclosure occurred in the termination phase of a successful analysis where the communication of the analyst's feelings was not used to perform a therapeutic function. The revelations did not occur in the context of a treatment impasse or the analyst's frustration with unrealized gains. I believe it is acceptable to momentarily dissolve the asymmetry at the end of a treatment when doing so for affectionate reasons and when the therapeutic work is largely completed. One indication that this condition is met revolves around the awareness that the disclosure is not meant to move the patient in some unfinished therapeutic direction. Nor is it meant to sidestep or circumvent important mourning. This is a difficult judgment call but one that will revolve around the analyst's awareness that the patient has demonstrated her/his acceptance of the limitations in the analytic relationship. It is crucial that this work has already been done.

Fourth, this patient is high functioning and especially so by the end of the analysis. In the vignette described above, the patient was capable (in the analyst's and my judgment) of receiving this communication without confusion and without becoming overstimulated. In other words, we surmised that he would be able to retain the 'I would if I could' sentiment, transitionality, or the 'as if' context, the persistently containing frame around the analyst's feelings for him.

Fifth, this supervisee was aware of the performative nature of words, i.e., words *do*, they are not passive, they are actions, and the revelation of erotic feelings, especially when mutual, is a form of foreplay. This was a reason for her disciplined restraint throughout the analysis and is linked to her assessment of the patient's ability to receive this communication without becoming confused now.

Sixth, all of these issues were being discussed in an ongoing and detailed way with a trusted supervisor, consultant, or peer group. The presence of supportive yet potentially correcting 'thirds' is a necessity as our capacity for self-deception is an ever-present corrupting potential.

Seventh, and finally, the analyst and supervisor(s)/consultant(s) agreed that the analyst was contained in terms of her personal needs. Monitoring our own personal needs for self-care is an ongoing responsibility, much like the need for musicians to have finely tuned instruments.

Final thoughts

I have had many patients who want to know how I feel about them. Sometimes this revolves specifically around my erotic feelings for them. They want me to 'touch' them with words as a symbol that I care for them in a personal way, beyond my professional role, and beyond their being my patient. "I need something concrete to let me know you really care for me," they might say in one way or another. The fantasy about the spoken word is that it is objectified, a *thing* that will *touch* them in a more palpable and lasting way than their silent speculations might.[10] But words have their own ambiguity and often do not last beyond the moment they are uttered.

I usually do not reciprocate a request for such signs of my caring, whether it be a loving or desiring phrase, a hug, or a meeting outside the office, but instead make it the very subject of a detailed analysis. Why do they need such an overt sign of my affection? Why is their ability to detect what I feel for them, in a personal, authentic way (not beyond my professional role but embedded within it) not speaking to them? Our focus becomes their overreliance on the concrete level of experience, overt expressions that indeed include words, in an effort to obtain an illusorily permanent reassurance that they are loved, wanted, or appreciated in a lasting way.

I remind them that any concrete sign or gesture will fall flat in the absence of a resonance with what they experience within our relationship on a feeling level. I remind my patients that words are at once ephemeral and ambiguous, that persons can lie with words in a way they cannot with feelings. I encourage my patients to explore what they know *based on what they feel* is between us so that words become unnecessary, even thin compared to the depth of attachment between us. It is as if the treatment is designed to hone their radar or antennae, directed at their own feelingful experience of the relationship, including and especially, what they sense I feel about them.

Notes

1 For a selection of readings on this controversial subject, see Davies (1994, 1998b, 2001); Gabbard (1994a, 1996, 1998, 2016); Cooper (1998); de Peyer (2002, 2022); Elise (2015, 2020); Hoffman (1998); Knoblauch (1995); Ehrenberg (1992); Renn (2013); Renik (1993); Hirsch (2008); Kuchuck (2012); Atlas (2013, 2016).

2 Who plead for love, and look for recompense
   More than that tongue that more hath express'd.
   O, learn to read what silent love hath writ
   To hear with eyes belongs to love's fine wit.
                    (W. Shakespeare, Sonnet 23, 1609)

3 It is always a risk to present clinical material out of context. For the serious reader, I encourage a full acquaintance with this material and its context by reading the entire articles cited herein.
4 Personal communication, October, 2013.
5 Before entertaining the possibility of a verbal, personal disclosure by the analyst, the reader is encouraged to revisit the description of the complexity of the analytic frame in Chapter 4 on mutuality and asymmetry.
6 Samuels (1985) speaks of the alchemical metaphor used by Jung in describing personality, dialogical 'fluids,' and the analytical 'container.'
7 In Atlas' case, the phrase referred to a third person. How much more saturated with meaning the phrase would be if it were uttered in relation to the two of them.
8 A testament, no doubt, to mutual right-hemisphere unconscious communications accounting for their unverbalized 'knowing' of each other (Schore, 2011).
9 As Slavin (2013) has succinctly put it, "The moment of truth [is] speaking the truth, *not* disclosing it" (p. 145, italics in original). Similarly, Bollas (1983) cautions that direct expression of countertransference, "must be experienced by the patient as a legitimate and natural part of the analytic process. If it comes as a shock then the analyst has failed in his technique" (p. 12).
10 See Celenza (2011) for a related discussion on touch in the analytic setting.

Chapter 7

Erotic transferences and sexual boundary violations[1]

It has been said that many analyses come to revolve around one basic question, "Why can't we be lovers?" Posed as a hypothetical, a 'what if' kind of mental exercise, this sometimes urgent question prompts the most useful exploration of the patient's deeply cherished wishes, longings, fantasies, and sexual desire. What happens, though, when this question does not remain at a hypothetical level? Is it then answered once and for all? Is there a therapeutic aspect to actualizing such deeply held longings? Why are there such strong prohibitions against sexual contact between analyst and patient? Why do sexual boundary violations occur, at a relatively high prevalence rate, it might be added, despite the strong prohibitions against them?

All disciplines in mental health practice consider sexual boundary violations the most egregious kind of ethical violation. Despite this, the problem has a long history and it has only been addressed in the last several decades. Many of Freud's inner circle became involved with one or more patients – Carl Jung with Sabina Spielrein, Sandor Ferenczi with Gizella and Elma Palos (mother *and* daughter, both of whom were patients), and Ernest Jones with Loë Kann, who eventually became his common-law wife. At one time or another, Freud was consulted, ostensibly to help disentangle the various boundary violations [see Gabbard and Lester (1995) and Kerr (1993) for historical reviews within psychoanalysis; Strean (1993) for an historical review in mental health professions in general].

Today, analysts and therapists who have sexually crossed boundaries are usually expelled from their professional organizations, lose their licensure, and typically lose the majority of their colleagues and friends along the way. Because the consequences are so grave, the

DOI: 10.4324/9781003391012-7

question is often posed, Why aren't analysts deterred by the threats of losing their livelihood, career, and social network? What is it that causes an analyst to violate boundaries in this most extreme way?

The answer to all of the questions posed above rests on an understanding of *how power issues and loving feelings intersect* in therapeutic settings. Among all mental health professionals, sexual boundary violations are recognized as unethical due to the power imbalance inherent in the structure of the relationship. This imbalance derives from many sources, but revolves primarily around the *unequal distribution of attention* paid to the analysand/patient.[2] The way in which the analyst acquires increasing knowledge of the patient articulates and enhances the power imbalance over time. The power that the analyst has is constituted by knowledge; in particular, the analyst's knowledge of the patient's inner life, her hopes, fears, shames, and longings.[3]

Definition

Sexual boundary violations are defined as any kind of physical contact occurring in the context of a psychoanalytic or therapeutic relationship *for the purpose of erotic pleasure*. It should be noted that there is touching that can, though rarely, occur in the context of treatment that would not be included in this definition. An occasional handshake or even a hug (for example, at termination), when the intent, at least on the analyst's part, is not erotic. Already, however, it is possible to see a difficulty in the attempt to distinguish one person's intent from another's conscious or unconscious hope or reaction. Many affectionate gestures made by analysts are misconstrued, either at the time they occur or at some later point. This is why any kind of physical touch in the therapeutic setting is for the most part discouraged.

Prevalence

I am unaware of recent prevalence studies, but those done in the last decades of the last century consistently revealed an unacceptably high incidence rate (7%–12%) of erotic contact between analysts and patients in the United States (Kardener et al., 1973; Holroyd and Brodsky, 1977; Pope et al., 1979; Gechtman and Bouhoutsos, 1985; Gartrell et al., 1986; Pope et al., 1986; Pope et al., 1987; Akamatsu, 1988; Borys and Pope, 1989; Lamb and Catanzaro, 1998; Jackson and Nuttall, 2001).

All of the studies cited above were comprised of anonymous, self-report questionnaires and most were derived from a national pool of various disciplines, including psychiatrists, psychologists, social workers, counselors, and/or clergy in the United States. Studies of British psychologists' self-reported prevalence reveal data similar to the studies in the United States (Garrett and Davis, 1998). Since all of these studies rely on the willingness of analysts and therapists to report on their own behavior, it is likely that the results underrepresent the true prevalence rate.

These studies generally show remarkable consistency in age, gender, and practice features. The typical transgressor is a middle-aged male analyst in solo private practice who engages in a sexual dual relationship with one female patient (Butler and Zelen, 1977; Pope et al., 1979; Bouhoutsos et al., 1983; Borys and Pope, 1989; Epstein et al., 1992; Lamb et al., 1994; Lamb and Catanzaro, 1998; Somer and Saadon, 1999; Jackson and Nuttall, 2001). Some studies have suggested that as analysts age and gain more experience, ethical judgment falls below previously held standards (Borys and Pope, 1989; Stake and Oliver, 1991; Epstein et al., 1992; Lamb et al., 1994; Rodolfa et al., 1994).

These studies also consistently show an overrepresentation of male analysts in those who report having engaged in sexual boundary violations. The statistics reflect 7%–9% male analysts while female analysts accounted for only 2%–3% of the incidence rate (Holroyd and Brodsky, 1977; Pope et al., 1979; Gartrell et al., 1986; Borys and Pope, 1989; Schoener et al., 1989; Parsons and Wincze, 1995; Jackson and Nuttall, 2001). In our clinical experience, Glen Gabbard and I[4] have the impression that the prevalence of female transgressors has risen as the field has recently become more feminized.

Interestingly, some preliminary data suggest that the female analysts who engage in sexual boundary violations with female patients are not necessarily self-identified as homosexual prior to their involvement with their patient. Benowitz (1995) studied 15 female therapists where sexual violations occurred with one female patient and found 20% of these therapists self-identified as heterosexual, 20% as bisexual, and 40% as clearly lesbian. Benowitz suggests that some female therapists use the relationship with the patient to explore their own sexuality.

The least frequent pairings are male analyst-male patient and female analyst-male patient. Gonsiorek (1989) found conflicts and insecurities revolving around sexual orientation in his study of male transgressors. One especially influential risk factor occurs when the analyst is in the throes of his or her own 'coming out' process.

Common characteristics

Previous clinical observations have culminated in a range of profiles and diagnostic categories of the transgressing therapist or analyst. Six diagnostic categories were delineated by Schoener and Gonsiorek (1989) including (1) uninformed/naive, (2) healthy or mildly neurotic, (3) severely neurotic and/or socially isolated, (4) impulsive character disorders, (5) sociopathic or narcissistic character disorders, and (6) psychotic or borderline personalities. A seventh category, bipolar disorders, was added in 1994 (Schoener, personal communication). Gabbard (1994b) proposed four underlying psychological profiles as an alternative classification scheme. These underlying characteristics include (1) psychotic disorders, (2) predatory psychopathy and paraphilias, (3) lovesickness, and (4) masochistic surrender. The last two categories, lovesick and masochistic surrender can be conceived as occupying two ends along the same continuum (Celenza and Gabbard, 2003).

Little is known about the psychology of the psychopathic predator because these transgressors typically refuse to be evaluated, persistently lie about the misconduct (even when multiple complaints are filed), and, if they lose their license to practice, still display no motivation to rehabilitate themselves. One such case involved over 20 complaints from former patients; the analyst continued to deny the abuse over several years as the many complainants came forward. So-called 'multiple offenders' tend to show no remorse or guilt and usually blame the patient for the seduction and transgression.

The dynamics of these psychopathically organized transgressors usually revolve around sadism and a need for power or control (Smith, 1984; Pope and Bouhoutsos, 1986; Celenza, 2006b, 2007). On superficial observation, this type of transgressor is described as charismatic, difficult (perhaps intimidating), and highly regarded, at least by some (see, for example, Sandler's (2004) depiction of Masud Khan). It is a sad fact that no profession has been wholly successful in weeding out these types of characters; indeed, it is a characteristic of the psychopathic personality to charm and mimic the behavior of a competent professional with great interpersonal skill (see Smith, 1984 for a description of several analyst/predators). After one or more complaints are filed and the practitioner loses his license, the psychopathic predator usually continues to practice as a "psychotherapist" as this vocation does not require licensure (in the U.S.).

The particularities of the women who become sexually involved with this type of analyst are not consequential in the understanding of psychopathic predation, i.e., in the selection by the transgressor of any one woman at any one time. The women are characteristically diverse, though objectified and interchangeable in the transgressor's mind, i.e., there is little recognition by the transgressor of the other as a separate subject. This is not to suggest that the psychopathic predator or 'multiple offender' does not have an intrapsychic personality organization that might be identified and described. However, we simply do not know (from a first-hand evaluative position) what the personality organization might be in terms of internal motivating conscious and unconscious dynamics. Because these offenders typically lose their license and are expelled from professional communities, they are lost to follow up. For these reasons, we remain unfamiliar with their underlying personality organization at a psychodynamic or psychoanalytic level.

Some speculation is unavoidable, however it is derived from behavioral observations and psychoanalytic theorizing. In this context, the following suggestions should be held lightly since they are not based on careful, comprehensive, and in-depth evaluations aided by first-person accounts or information derived from in-depth treatments. (This is in direct contrast to the incisive knowledge we have gleaned from the intensive evaluations and in-depth treatments of the one-time offenders, summarized below.) With regard to psychopathic predators, the behavior manifested in their relationships with the victims reflects the experience of the other as de-particularized and objectified, as noted above. We can presume that this refers to a primitive level of intrapsychic organization, i.e., relating to others as part-objects, absent of subjectivity, and used for (sexual) sensation rather than through a more meaningful intersubjective involvement. Given the absence of or hope for some kind of unconscious repair, these relationships lead to seemingly endless repetition of similar engagements, hence the tendency toward multiple victims.

In some cases, it can be discerned that the exploitation is driven primarily by the predator's desire to degrade the industry/profession. As I have noted elsewhere (Celenza, 2022c),

> Other sexual boundary transgressions, especially the most notorious, predatory type, can make use of a displacement object, [the dynamics of which] are more accurately formulated as a *displaced perverse scenario*. In these cases of sexual boundary transgressions, the effort to degrade is often not primarily directed at the [victim] but is directed at the profession, the body or figure that, in fantasy, oversees the dyad. Hence the frequent use of the symbol of the couch, the icon of psychoanalysis, as a place to enact this scenario.[5]

In this sense, the couch can be viewed as a third[6] symbolically representative of psychoanalysis. *The patient is a displacement object*, a stand-in, so to speak, for an aspect of the setting or context. In displaced perverse scenarios, the primary motivation is the erasure or degradation of the third.[7]

From another vertex, the sparseness in the literature on psychopathic predators may reflect a more clinically meaningful phenomenon. It is possible that this 'negative space' is a dynamically meaningful absence, that is, a *present absence* reflecting unrepresented, nonverbal areas in the psyche of these persons. The disturbing externalizations typical of these individuals usually indicate defensive processes likely borne from trauma and reflective of deficits in the capacity to mentalize and internalize conflicts manifested in their acting-out. Perhaps we can look beyond these behavioral observations and speculate, not that they *refuse* to be evaluated, but that they *cannot* be evaluated, that is, cannot feel or take responsibility due to the inability to self-reflect, mentalize, and thereby be known at a meaningful level. Again, speculatively, we could wonder whether the externalizing and projective defenses are those more familiarly associated with deficits at a structural level, i.e., the turbulence of the unstructured unconscious, rather than conflicts representative of structured, albeit repressed fantasies and wishes.

Most analyst/transgressors are not psychopathic predators. In the mental health field, and I suggest especially among psychoanalytic therapists and psychoanalysts, research consistently shows that *the great majority of sexual boundary violators are one-time offenders who exploit one patient, usually over a period of time where the phenomenal, conscious experience is one of a mutual rescue fantasy and an idealized, romantic love*. Though the truth is more complicated and revealed over time (perhaps only with subsequent treatment), the idealized love is inarguably exploitative and thereby unhealthy from the beginning. Still, it is most often consciously experienced as a 'true' love affair by both victim and transgressor.

Though the patients may ultimately feel objectified and used (as in psychopathic predation), the tragic truth is that these patient/victims usually do represent an *unconsciously meaningful other* to the analyst/ transgressor in very particularized ways. By and large, the relationship, from the analyst/therapist's point of view, engages a grandiose attempt to provide a cure through the purity of their (incestuous) love. I insert the word incestuous here because of the power imbalance, inevitably conjuring the parent-child generational difference and also evoking, for these transgressors, a transferential opportunity to reinstate an unresolved, fantasied omnipotent position of the son (now analyst/ therapist) in relation to a depressed and unreachable maternal figure. Not coincidentally, the paternal figure or third is nowhere to be found in this psychic scenario. These women are not objectified and inter- changeable (as they are with psychopathic predation) but are very spe- cific transference objects to the analyst, harkening back to unresolved childhood internalized imagoes.[8]

There are typical features and a common scenario associated with this most prevalent type of sexual misconduct (Plakun, 1999; Celenza and Gabbard, 2003; Celenza, 2007). The scenario most often involves a heterosexual male analyst who becomes sexually involved with only one of his patients.[9] The analyst is usually mid-career, isolated in his practice and is treating a difficult patient in a highly stressful time in his life. The relationship is usually intense, may last for several years and the couple may feel that they have found 'true love,' at least ini- tially. Sometimes the treatment relationship is terminated while the sexual relationship continues. If the relationship is brought to an end by the analyst, this is the time when an ethical complaint is most likely to be filed by the patient.

There are several common characteristics that have been identi- fied related to the analyst's personality, life circumstance, past history, and the transference/countertransference dynamics of this particular analyst-patient pair (Gonsiorek and Schoener, 1987; Twemlow and Gabbard, 1989; Celenza, 1998, 2007, 2011). These are presented be- low (see Table 7.1). While certain precursors may be longstanding, most researchers have found these analysts capable of conducting competent and ethical treatment for most of their professional career (Gabbard and Lester, 1995). For this type of transgressor, the greatest risk involves a particular transference/countertransference (mis)fit at a highly stressful time of their lives. Erotic transferences, manifested in a negative, frustrating, and sometimes volatile manner by the patient, present a particularly difficult but frequent challenge to the analyst.

The following precursors are presented not as a way to differentiate ourselves from transgressors but to recognize the potential transgressor in all of us. Though there is a ubiquitous temptation to apply an 'us-them' type of disclaiming to these characteristics and warning signs, I have found that it is the analyst who insists s/he is not at risk who is most vulnerable.

There are eight risk factors that have been identified that may represent precursors to sexual boundary violations (Celenza, 1998, 2007, 2011). The first involves **longstanding and unresolved narcissistic neediness** and lifelong struggles with low self-esteem and depression. Almost all therapists reported ongoing struggles with a sense of unworthiness, inadequacy, or outright feelings of failure throughout their lives. These therapists tended to rely on their patients to meet their narcissistic needs and required that their patients always hold them in positive esteem. Many patients reported a sense that angry or disappointed feelings toward the therapist or the treatment were taboo.

These therapists do not appear to be overtly arrogant or grandiose (like the charismatic psychopathic predator); rather, they display **a covert and denied grandiosity** (the second precursor) that is apparent in their fantasies and ideals. Observation usually reveals a mild-mannered, self-effacing, and humble exterior that hides underlying (and unchallenged) beliefs in powers of rescue and omnipotence. Upon close examination of their clinical practices, there are usually many

Table 7.1 Precursors of Sexual Boundary Violations[a]

- Longstanding narcissistic vulnerability
- Grandiose (covert) rescue fantasies
- Intolerance of negative transference
- Childhood history of emotional deprivation and sexualized overstimulation
- Family history of covert and sanctioned boundary transgressions
- Unresolved anger toward authority figures
- Restricted awareness of fantasy (especially hostile/aggressive)
- Transformation of countertransference hate to countertransference love

[a] n > 50 cases of therapist sexual misconduct in the context of evaluation, therapy, supervision, or consultation (Celenza, 1998, 2007, 2011).

slippery slope boundary crossings with unusually challenging patients. Indeed, these therapists often pride themselves in being able to treat the untreatable and to do so in unconventional ways.

The third precursor is described as an ***intolerance of negative transference*** in these therapists. This risk factor is not necessarily particular to the therapist-patient dyad in which the exploitation occurred but can be characteristic of their treatment style in general. Most likely due to the fragility in self-esteem, this group of transgressors has great difficulty tolerating and exploring disappointments, frustrations, and/ or criticisms that the patient may have about the treatment. Other transgressors, however, do not show a particular fragility in this area, conduct thorough explorations of negative transference with the large majority of their patients but are highly sensitive to criticism from the patient with whom he eventually transgresses.

The fourth precursor is comprised of two separate but related characteristics in the childhood history of the transgressor. These therapists report ***a sexualization in their relationship with the primary caregiver***. The data here does not refer to outright sexual abuse, but rather an overstimulation of the child in a sexualized manner, a kind of covert seductiveness that, most importantly, occurred against a background of ***emotional deprivation and neglect***. Their childhood is described as one where early needs for recognition, affirmation, attention, and affection were not met, leaving the child needy of these kinds of contact and attention.

Fifth, there is usually precedence in the family history of ***boundary transgressions by parental figure(s)***. This occurs against a background of high moralism and represents a denied hypocrisy. Family members may be aware of this hypocrisy. Wishes were simultaneously prohibited yet covertly permitted in a denied, unintegrated way.

It is easy to see how such a family situation may set the stage for the internalization of *vertically split superego structures* (one aspect of which is based on an identification with the transgressing parent) which *prohibits overt need gratification yet permits the gratification of wishes in secret and forbidden contexts*. The child develops a dual mode of moral functioning (or a split in superego structures) based on an identification with both levels of functioning in the parent(s). Thus, reality consists of two levels: one that is moral and consensual but restrictive and depriving while another is secret, compartmentalized, and immoral. It is in this latter level of reality where forbidden needs may be gratified. This dynamic may mirror the patient's wish to reenact a sexual relationship with a forbidden object with which the therapist then colludes (Gabbard, 1994b). The identification with the transgressing parent includes permitting the gratification of wishes in secret, forbidden contexts. The therapeutic setting is one such context.

Sixth, there is usually intense and unconscious **unresolved anger toward authority figures**. Though they often can present themselves as highly remorseful (which is genuine), the exploitation itself represents a rebellion against the authority of their profession and an underlying desire to break the rules. Derived from unresolved anger toward the authoritarian parent, the licensing board, ethics committees, and/or professional organization can come to represent these authority figures. Among psychoanalysts who have transgressed, Gabbard (1994a) and Gabbard and Lester (1995) have found evidence of unresolved anger or resentment at the institute or training analyst with a concomitant fantasy of embarrassing these authority figures by disgracing oneself.

Seventh, **restricted awareness of fantasy** was observed in a majority of the therapists, especially in those who presented with genuine guilt and self-reproach. This restriction is evident in both sexual and aggressive realms where the therapist is unable to admit to or access hateful or desirous wishes except in conventional or muted ways. Notably, most also had great difficulty acknowledging the transgressions as inherently hostile.

The last factor involves a **circumventing of unconscious countertransference hate through the misuse of conscious countertransference 'love'**. This is a defensive process triggered in part by the therapist's intolerance of his or her own aggression. The defensive circumventing of countertransference hate was particularly related to the therapist's inability to view him/herself as depriving or non-nurturant. These therapists tended to emphasize supportive and guiding views of therapy, over-relying on the so-called `corrective emotional experience.'

For female transgressors, the great majority of patient/victims are female (roughly two thirds). As noted, these transgressors are not necessarily previously self-identified as gay. The typical dynamic scenario in these cases is also not characterized by psychopathic predation where the other (i.e., the patient/victim) is an interchangeable object, but rather comprises a very particularized reenactment that is unconsciously meaningful to each. The exploitation is again a mutual rescue fantasy, however from the point of view of the female analyst/transgressor, it is an *over-identification with the patient in a highly idealized fashion*. One female analyst said to me, "She was the child I was.

I couldn't stand the pain she was in. I had to help her out of this pain."
This experience reflects the subjective, phenomenal experience as well
as unconscious, intrapsychic meanings that the relationship has for the
analyst. The relationship is also characterized by a stark disregard for
differences between the analyst and patient, including an almost total
neglect of the patient's aggression.

From our clinical work, Glen Gabbard and I[10] have the impression
that the types of predation have changed (discussed further below),
but it is generally safe to assume that sexual boundary violations of at
least one sort (the so-called one-time offender) will never be eradicated
and is best understood as an occupational hazard. Because practitioners (especially psychoanalytic) have actively sought to address the
problem of sexual boundary violations since the late 1980s, there is
now zero-tolerance for psychopathic predation and I surmise this has
resulted in a markedly lower frequency of this type of exploitation.
However, as noted above, the frequency of one-time offenders has not
declined and there is a discernable rise in female transgressors.

What can be said about the victims of sexual boundary violations
outside of the transgressor's perspective, especially in relation to the
question of whether there is a characteristic profile or cluster of qualities that are typically found? There is one characteristic (actually a
positive and healthy quality) that most, if not all, victims possess and
that is the tendency to care for others, to empathically perceive the
other's point of view, and to provide the care they sense is needed.
Sadly, this can play a part in reversing roles. As for other characteristics that may play a meaningful role in the dyadic enactment, these are
particularized and do not fall into neat categories.

Precursors contextualized in the therapy relationship

The structure of the treatment situation is a template that replicates
several of the familial dynamics outlined above. The therapeutic
context is essentially a depriving situation for the analyst in that it
is asymmetric. The patient is the recipient of the attention paid and
whose psychological and therapeutic needs are met. In contrast, it is
the analyst's responsibility to put his needs aside for most of the hours
in his day. For an analyst who experienced emotional deprivation in
childhood, the treatment situation can perilously replicate this early
deprivation.

At the same time, the treatment situation may be overstimulating to the analyst in that the content of many therapy hours can involve intensely sexualized material. Here, the treatment situation replicates another childhood trauma and taken together, the emotional surround is one that is simultaneously depriving and sexually overstimulating. It is also a context where it is overtly forbidden for the analyst to gain gratification of his wishes, paralleling the prohibitive atmosphere in these analysts' childhood experience.

These treatments have a bi-modal trajectory where the first phase is idealizing, possibly characterized by a positive, maternal erotic transference. As the analysand or patient progresses, she becomes increasingly frustrated with the hierarchical, asymmetric structure of the setting and a negative erotic transference emerges. These are usually intense moments or phases and with certain patients, this part of the treatment may escalate into a crisis and/or include threats of suicide (Wheelis et al., 2003), self-mutilation, or even blackmail. These and other kinds of implicit and explicit threats can render the analyst (subjectively) helpless and desperate (Gutheil and Gabbard, 1992, 1993, 1998; Gabbard, 1994b, 2016; Celenza, 1998, 2007, 2011). *Because of the analyst's narcissistic fragility, he may be moved to transform the nature of the therapeutic process at this phase, relying on sexualization to transform the way in which the patient is responding to him* (see, for example, Eyman and Gabbard, 1991; Celenza and Gabbard, 2003; Gabbard, 2003). He may enact a masochistic scenario, linked to childhood wishes of self-sacrifice and "going out in a blaze of glory" by acting on incestuous wishes and courting punishment for the forbidden act of pleasure (Gabbard and Lester, 1995). Searles (1979) put it well in stating, "[The analyst] has succumbed to the illusion that a magically curative copulation will resolve the patient's illness" (p. 431).

Thus, the seduction occurs when the analyst believes that the therapy is at an impasse. In this way, the process shifts from one of enormous frustration and challenge to one of seduction and sexual gratification. One analyst revealingly said, "I was reaching the end of my rope. I didn't know how to help her. I knew how to seduce her, so that's what I did."

Does he really love me?

One of the most vexing, persistent, and painful sequelae of the particular post-traumatic stress syndrome associated with sexual boundary violations is directly derived from the corruption of the asymmetric structure of the treatment. When the asymmetry is corrupted, the betrayal is not the sex, or even the love itself, but *the lie*, the use of the treatment (perversely) *for the analyst*, when the contract (and promise) was for the patient. The problem is not the love, unhealthy, incestuous, and asymmetric as it is, but the broken promise upon which the treatment now rests. This, then, challenges the patient/victim with an impossible task – *to believe in a love that rests upon a broken covenant.* The aftermath of sexual boundary violations revolves around this insecure foundation, where patient/victims are tortured by a lingering, persistent, and profound inner doubt of the verity and realness of love.

For the patient/victim, this then becomes a pervasive doubt – transformed into a seemingly unresolvable question, "Did he *really* love me?" Despite clear memories of having been told, in both words and deed, that she is loved ("But he said he loved me, why can't I believe it?"), there is always a profound inner doubt that lingers in their mind. Paradoxically, it is usually the doubt about her lovability that formed a conscious rationale for the transgression in the first place. Indeed, often enough it was the analyst's conscious purpose, in violating boundaries, to show her once and for all that she is *really* loved. And of course, this was usually the reason for her seeking treatment initially.

This persistent doubt about whether the transgressor *really* loved the patient/victim is based on two conceptual problems, the first being confusion over the essential nature of love in the analytic setting and its quality of realness (see Celenza, 2022, Essay #1). The second conceptual problem is the question of what exactly is the nature of the betrayal in sexual boundary transgressions. Is it the sexual exploitation? Is it indeed the sex? I am suggesting that the fundamental violation, and the most painful disillusionment, is a *particular lie*, inherent in the violation itself and sometimes stated explicitly, "This is for you." Every sexual boundary violation includes such a lie as part of the perversion of the asymmetric treatment contract, though the analyst may deny, rationalize, or justify such a means/end reversal.[11]

The treatment contract revolves around a promise to preserve the analytic pre-symbolic space for the work of expanding meaning construction. This promise is actualized through the roles each member plays, most importantly by the analyst in maintaining the asymmetric distribution of attention, focus, and care. In the case of sexual boundary violations, however, it is through this broken promise that the analyst conveys his/her capacity to lie, to have made a promise that is not kept, and perhaps was never meant. Having done this, nothing built on top of this lie will resonate as true.

For those transferences that arise from within the analytic setting, the promise is to analyze and thereby foster understanding, especially from a psychoanalytic perspective, and to do that *and only that*. For this reason, transferences emerge with great intensity, having been invited and seduced by the promise of maintaining the structure and safety of the setting. Morris (2012) refers to this as, "the enabling *constitutive disavowal* of the analytic setting," i.e., the promise to maintain an illusory separation between analysis and external life.

By virtue of having made this promise, our patients take more risks revealing their desires in bald and undefended form. Through the embodiment of our role, we continually assert, "You are not obliged to me." This is why the exploitation of these revelations for the analyst's own purposes is particularly perverse.

As analysts, we continually make this commitment in a self-state that is restrained in terms of our separate desires and needs. Because of this promise, to restrain our own desire, we invite the emergence of unrestrained, relatively undefended desires of the patient. We are particularly inviting of pre-symbolic, unmetabolized affects and desires, the unknown, secret, perhaps shame-inducing aspects of the other's longings that have yet to be symbolized. It is in this context of the promise, the commitment to asymmetry, that the invitation to desire and the desire itself emerges and is intensified, due to the promise of presence without repercussion, obligation, or consequence. The promise seduces desire to emerge and intensify, to express itself in its fullest passion and complexity. We promise and thereby evoke faith, trust, and belief in our strength and integrity, that we will maintain our awareness of separateness and inhibition of our own desires and needs; in short, that we will keep our word.

Therefore, the question is not, Did he *really* love me (or was he lying about loving me)? but, Is this love healthy and growth-promoting (or an unhealthy repetition of past imbalanced loves)? A healthy love includes a mutual, symmetrical love where power imbalances are negotiable. This is in direct contrast to the asymmetrical love evoked in the analytic setting which is, by definition, based on a variety of structured (and thereby non-negotiable) power imbalances, as in oedipal transferences. Further, it is an unhealthy love because it is rooted in a broken covenant and thereby has sown the seeds of mistrust.

Common misconceptions

It is very important for analysts to be aware of the warning signs and particular vulnerabilities associated with the problem of sexual boundary violations. The misconceptions that surround this problem prevent analysts from adequately addressing these vulnerabilities before it is too late. Consultation, supervision, and regular discussion in peer study groups are often absent as potential sources of support in cases of sexual boundary transgressions. The punitive atmosphere within the profession, including licensing boards, ethics committees, and over-seeing professional agencies, also engender a prohibitive atmosphere that creates an additional barrier to analysts seeking help when they need it.

There is a tendency for most analysts to disown the problem, supported by the belief that analysts who engage in sexual boundary viola-tions are psychopathic and/or grandiose, i.e., fundamentally different from ourselves (Celenza and Gabbard, 2003). This allows analysts to deny their own vulnerability to this problem. Through the use of a variety of defenses such as splitting, disavowal, and projection, many analysts attempt to console themselves that sexual boundary violations could never happen to them because they are educated, ethical, and well-intended.

It is dangerous to hold the belief that one is immune to this type of boundary transgression because those who continue to deny their own vulnerability will be more likely to ignore warning signs and less likely to seek help and support. It is also more likely that aspects of self-care will be underappreciated, since most analysts who have become sexu-ally involved with a patient do so at a stressful time in their lives. Knowing the ethical code surrounding the maintenance of appropriate boundaries is not a safeguard against boundary violations since the great majority of transgressors do so knowing full well that they are violating the ethical code of their profession.

The absence of sexual attraction toward a particular patient also does not safeguard against sexual exploitation. This is another com-mon misunderstanding of the problem itself and a way in which sexual boundary violations are commonly portrayed in film. In real life, sex-ual boundary violations are not about a physically appealing patient or a romantic/sexual spark between two people. When the transgressor is a psychopathic predator, he may select particularly attractive and ap-pealing patients among his entourage. However, in the most prevalent kind of sexual boundary violation, the seduction is most often the result of a defensive reaction to a difficult patient at a stressful time in the analyst's life. It is most common to hear the transgressor say (in retrospect), "I never thought I'd be sexual with any patient and certainly not with this one."

I have not found any differences between analysts versus therapists with regard to the characteristics discussed above. This has been surprising, given the amount of training and the depths of treatment(s) analysts presumably have undergone. I would have imagined greater insulation among analysts against masochistic surrender as well as less narcissistic vulnerability to engaging in sexual boundary violations. Barring both of these, I expected at least a greater understanding of their dynamics and intrapsychic (perhaps even unconscious) vulnerabilities to certain kinds of enactments, related to their personal histories. This is sadly not the case. On the contrary, I have been surprised at the lack of insight into their involvement with the patient and their 'love' for her.

Instead, what I have discovered is a specific kind of *unidimensional thinking* about the transgression, even somewhat concretized and unsymbolized. Given that the analyst embodies multiple self-states in relation to the patient, we know that the multiplicity of roles can collapse under the pressure of undue desire or need. The perplexity we often feel when a previously competent, even revered analyst comes to describe his role in relation to his patient in an oversimplified, justifying manner is stunning both in its distortion of the process, but especially for its unidimensionality and oversimplification. The retreat from role or disciplined commitment involves the truncating of self-states, the erasure of other potential modes of being, and a psychic shift from analyst-as-multiple to analyst-as-(solely) lover. Here, the boundaries have become impermeable and define a unidimensional mode of relating that is constricted by the retreat from, walling off of, or erasure of other potentialities.

Only upon subsequent treatment and in-depth reflection do these transgressions become more fully elaborated and explained. Many analyst/transgressors have noted deficits in their prior analysis (sometimes analys*es*) while others have regarded the transgression as inevitable given life circumstances and the like.

I have also not found differences in prevalence among the different psychoanalytic orientations. *Our theories fail us differently.* Our theories all fail us, but in different ways, so there actually may be some differentiations to be made in type of sexual boundary transgression and profile (correlated with theoretical orientation), but not in quantity or frequency of occurrence.[12]

Concluding remarks

Loving feelings are inevitably stirred up in the treatment context, especially in psychoanalysis. Love and erotic desire are the foundation of the work we do. Because of the defining structure of the treatment setting, however, and its inherent power imbalances, erotic contact is exploitative of the patient's vulnerability, even when sexual contact is consciously desired by the patient. In this time of technological advancements, telehealth, and other modes of conducting treatment, it is important to remember that the telehealth screen does not prevent feelings from being evoked. On the contrary, telehealth can provide an important transitional space that for some persons, allows for a deeper, more intense involvement of which they might otherwise be incapable. There is no safeguard against erotic transferences and erotic countertransferences. Indeed, these should be a part of every thorough-going analysis, nor are there safeguards against our capacity for self-deception, and conscious and unconscious desires to transgress limits (Samuels, 1996; Slochower, 1999, 2003, 2015, 2024; Saketopoulou, 2019, 2020).

Changes in our industry implicate and occur within the context of the sociocultural milieu of the setting, especially its cultural life. Features of our culture are clearly problematic and need to be addressed at this level. One example in the psychoanalytic ethos is its tendency toward overwork and the neglect of self-care (Celenza, 2007, 2010, 2022b), a feature of our grandiosity that is facilitated at the cultural level but instantiated differently at the individual level. This cultural trend sorely needs to be examined and addressed. Many colleagues have written or are writing about phenomena at this level: Glen Gabbard (2016), Adrienne Harris (2008), Muriel Dimen (2021), Avgi Saketopoulou (2020, 2021), Katie Gentile (2021), Julie Leavitt (2017), Jane Burka (2014), and multiple colleagues at the Psychoanalytic Institute of Northern California (Burka et al., 2019).

These authors have identified aspects of our sociocultural surround, especially in psychoanalytic institutes, that serve to contribute if not instigate sexual boundary violations among its members. In my view, these problematic dynamics include the pathologization of erotic countertransference (Celenza, 2014, 2022b; Saketopoulou, 2020), the intergenerational transmission of unrepresented, uncontained sexuality (Leavitt, 2017), the persistent desexualization of psychoanalytic theorizing (Celenza, 2014, 2022a, 2022b), the resistance to recognizing sexual boundary violations as a universal fallibility (Celenza, 2007, 2011), the tendency to polarize, vilify, and ultimately 'expel' the universal vulnerability to sexual boundary violations (Celenza and Gabbard, 2003; Celenza, 2007, 2011; Gabbard, 2016), and the lack of containment of such vulnerabilities extant in the psychoanalytic institutional milieu (Gabbard et al., 2001; Celenza, 2007, 2022a,c; Gabbard, 2016). Indeed, Leavitt (2017) sees the sociocultural surround of our psychoanalytic institutes as *already collaterally damaged* and thereby unable to provide a holding function.

Despite this, we must not be afraid to let our bodies experience the analytic process, to be present to our patients in our totality, including allowing sexual desire to be present in our countertransference. If we accept the universal vulnerability to sexual boundary violations, we might be tempted to retreat, thereby constraining our analytic stance. But this would mean a retreat from our patients who often need to speak frankly about their sexuality and to re-experience this aspect of their being with us, the object that cannot be had. If we constrain ourselves, desexualize our being in relation to our patients, and desexualize our theorizing as well, our patients will have nowhere else to go. Our work is threatening and difficult, precisely because the psychoanalytic setting is one where the analyst, as the forbidden incestuous object, is at once titillated and overstimulated while also constantly frustrated through our abiding disciplined stance. This is a set-up and frustration for us as well as our patients that requires the utmost ethical responsivity.

We need to have the full range of potent affectivity at our disposal. Not only is aggression a part of erotic transferences, it is implicated in *erotic countertransferences* as well. Analysts must function in their work as relatively integrated and capable of responding to the wide range of human suffering and joys.

To hold in mind the ubiquity of the erotic in our psychoanalytic project, indeed within the erotic field, is to remind us of the magnitude of our ethical stance and required discipline. This asymmetry is not a given but is comprised of moment-to-moment choices that require constant monitoring against a background of self-care (Celenza, 2016, 2017, 2022a, 2022b). There is a universal vulnerability to sexual boundary violations – of this I am convinced – and therefore, we must not pathologize erotic countertransference or view the absence of erotic feeling as a relief or an easy route to neutrality and abstinence. Rather, the absence of erotic arousal in our countertransference should be viewed as *a present absence* and in this way, problematized. The project of psychoanalysis is to strengthen subjectivity, heal divisions and splits, and co-construct subjectivities. This is a creative journey that requires both sexuality and aggression.

Most importantly, it is grandiose to believe we know what mental state awaits us as we age and face mortality. We may not be at risk for sexual transgressions at this moment in time, but we cannot know how capable and disciplined we will be in the future.

Power is an individual challenge as well as one that may be institutionally or hierarchically conferred. It does not translate into the 'powers that be' or 'received wisdom' but rather true power that has many registers. There is subjective power, that is the power that one owns and authorizes as a feature of one's personality. This is an aspect of one's subjectivity that we can consciously experience. Then there is another register in which power resides – this is the power that is structuralized. It is a kind of institutional power that is conferred (by both parties) by virtue of one's role in a particular context and the agreed-upon treatment contract.

The difference between subjective power and structuralized power is an important one because practitioners of all mental health disciplines are often confused by the so-called power imbalance inherent in the therapeutic setting. An analyst or therapist does not necessarily experience structuralized power on conscious, phenomenal levels. In fact, in the midst of the perfect storm of sexual boundary violations, the analyst/therapist often feels, consciously, that they have little to no power.

Idealization prevents metabolizing the disillusionments with our mentors (some of whom have become transgressors). This conflicts with the vision of the omnipotent analyst working 60 hours per week. In effect, we cherish our ideals more than we do our self-care. We must emphasize community as part of self-care – made up of trusted others with whom we can reveal our clinical errors. This includes supervisors who will not react punitively if we share erotic countertransferences (Slochower, 2024). This community (preferably, small groups) is not just any community but one that accepts our various occupational hazards (other-centeredness, self-deprivation, fantasies of rescue, depletion, burnout, and omnipotence) and can hold such clinical hazards as inevitable sequelae of inordinate dedication and isolation.

One of the salutary effects of our efforts in this vein inheres in the fact that therapists and analysts are coming forward more frequently for consultation and support when they fear they *might* become sexually involved with a patient. What better outcome could we hope for?

Notes

1 For a thorough explication of many of the issues discussed in this chapter, see Celenza (2007, 2011).
2 For ease of discussion, I will refer to the analyst or therapist and analysand or patient to represent the template for a relationship that contains a structured power imbalance.
3 See Chapter 4 for a more thorough discussion of the dialectic of mutuality and asymmetry that structures the treatment contract.
4 Personal communication, August, 2021.
5 For one clergy transgressor, the iconic symbol of his profession was the altar whereupon he was able to "fuck God and fuck the church at the same time" (Celenza, 2007, p. 44).
6 The term, third object, as used here, is differentiated from some of the ways in which the concept of the third is used in contemporary psychoanalytic theory (see Benjamin, 2004; Britton, 2004; Hanly, 2004 for helpful reviews). In the present discussion, the use of the third object is to be rigorously distinguished from the intersubjective third or symbolic third in that there is no recognition of a separate subjectivity in the mind of the transgressor. Rather, the third is used as in Benjamin's (2004) 'negative third' in complementarity or doer/done to relations, as Ogden's subjugating third (1994), or the way in which Greenberg (1999) and Spezzano (1998) use the concept, as representative of the analytic community.
7 See Celenza (2021) for a detailed discussion of the different modalities of defense associated with this and other profiles.
8 Needless to say, the analyst/transgressors retain full responsibility for the exploitation, and yet despite this, the dynamics reveal significant characteristics of the other that play a part in the unconscious scenario.
9 For ease of discussion, I will refer to the transgressor as 'he' or 'the analyst' and the patient as 'she' or 'the patient,' because this is the most frequent gender pairing.
10 Personal communication, August, 2021.
11 See Celenza (2022, Essay 31, *Perversion and its qualities of being*) for a discussion of perversion in this context.
12 See Celenza (2022, Essay 11, *Sexual boundary violations and theoretical orientation*) for more detail on this subject.

References

Akamatsu, T.J. (1988). Intimate relationships with former clients: National survey of attitudes and behavior among practitioners. *Professional Psychology: Research and Practice*, 19, 454–458.

Akhtar, S. (2009). *Comprehensive Dictionary of Psychoanalysis*. London: Karnac.

Aron, L. (1996). *A Meeting of Minds: Mutuality in Psychoanalysis*. Northvale, NJ: Analytic Press.

Atlas, G. (2013). What's love got to do with it? Sexuality, shame, and the use of the other. *Studies in Gender and Sexuality*, 14, 51–58.

Atlas, G. (2016). *The Enigma of Desire: Sex, Longing, and Belonging in Psychoanalysis*. New York: Routledge.

Balsam, R.M. (2001). Integrating male and female elements in a woman's gender identity. *Journal American Psychoanalytic Association*, 49, 1335–1360.

Balsam, R.M. (2003). The vanished pregnant body in psychoanalytic female developmental theory. *Journal American Psychoanalytic Association*, 51, 1153–1179.

Balsam, R.M. (2008). Women showing off: Notes on female exhibitionism. *Journal American Psychoanalytic Association*, 56, 99–121.

Balsam, R.M. (2012). *Women's Bodies in Psychoanalysis*. New York: Routledge.

Balsam, R.H. (2014). The embodied mother: Commentary on Kristeva. *Journal American Psychoanalytic Association*, 62(1), 87–100.

Balsam, R.H. (2019). On the natal body and its confusing place in mental life. *Journal American Psychoanalytic Association*, 67(1), 15–36.

Bassin, D. (1996). Beyond the he and the she: Toward the reconciliation of masculinity and femininity in the postoedipal female mind. *Journal American Psychoanalytic Association*, 44S, 157–190.

Benjamin, J. (1994b). Commentary on papers by Tansey, Davies, and Hirsch. *Psychoanalytic Dialogues*, 4, 193–201.

Benjamin, J. (1995). *Like Subjects, Love Objects*. New Haven, CT: Yale University Press.

Benjamin, J. (1997). Psychoanalysis as a vocation. *Psychoanalytic Dialogues*, 7, 781–802.

Benjamin, J. (1998). *Shadow of the Other: Intersubjectivity and Gender in Psychoanalysis*. New York: Routledge.

Benjamin, J. (2004). Beyond doer and done to: An intersubjective view of thirdness. *Psychoanalytic Quarterly*, 73, 5–46.

Benowitz, M. (1995). Comparing the experiences of women clients sexually exploited by female versus male psychotherapists. In J. Gonsiorek (Ed.), *A Breach of Trust: Sexual Exploitation by Health Care Professionals and Clergy* (pp. 213–224). London: Sage.

Bion, W.R. (1970). *Attention and Interpretation*. London: Tavistock.

Birksted-Breen, D. (1996). Unconscious representation of femininity. *Journal American Psychoanalytic Association*, 44(s), 119–132.

Bollas, C. (1983). Expressive uses of the countertransference: Notes to the patient from oneself. *Contemporary Psychoanalysis*, 19, 1–33.

Bollas, C. (1989). *The Shadow of the Object: Psychoanalysis of the Unthought Known*. New York: Columbia University Press.

Bollas, C. (1994). Aspects of the erotic transference. *Psychological Inquiry*, 14, 573–590.

Bolognini, S. (1994). Transference: Erotised, erotic, loving, affectionate. *International Journal Psychoanalysis*, 75, 73–86.

Bolognini, S. (2011). The analyst's awkward gift: Balancing recognition of sexuality with parental protectiveness. *Psychoanalytic Quarterly*, LXXX, 33–54.

Borys, D.S. and Pope, K.S. (1989). Dual relationships between therapist and client: A national study of psychologists, psychiatrists, and social workers. *Professional Psychology: Research and Practice*, 20, 283–293.

Bouhoutsos, J., Holroyd, J., Lerman, H., Forer, B., and Greenberg, J. (1983). Sexual intimacy between psychotherapists and patients. *Professional Psychology*, 14, 185–196.

Brady, M.T. (2022). Braving the erotic field in the treatment of adolescents. In M.T. Brady (Ed.), *Braving the Erotic Field in the Psychoanalytic Treatment of Children and Adolescents* (pp. 26–46). London: Routledge.

Britton, R. (1992). The Oedipus situation and the depression position. *New Library of Psychoanalysis*, 14, 34–45.

Britton, R. (2004). Subjectivity, objectivity, and triangular space. *Psychoanalytic Quarterly*, 73, 47–61.

Burka, J. (2014). A chorus of difference: Evolving from moral outrage to complexity and pluralism. In R.A. Deutsche (Ed.), *Traumatic Ruptures: Abandonment and Betrayal in the Analytic Relationship* (pp. 126–143). New York: Routledge.

Burka, J., Sowa, A., Baer, B., Brandes, C., Gallup, J., Karp-Lewis, S., Leavitt, J., and Rosbrow, P. (2019). From the talking cure to a disease of silence: Effects of ethical violations in a psychoanalytic institute. *International Journal Psychoanalysis*, 100(2), 247–271.

Butler, J. (1995). Melancholy gender—Refused identification. *Psychoanalytic Dialogues*, 5, 165–180.

Butler, S. and Zelen, S.L. (1977). Sexual intimacies between therapists and clients. *Psychotherapy: Theory, Research and Practice*, 14(2), 139–145.

Cartwright, M. (2016). *World History Encyclopedia*. https://www.ancient.eu/atlantis/.

Celenza A. (1998). Precursors to therapist sexual boundary violations: Preliminary findings. *Psychoanalytic Psychology*, 15, 378–395.

Celenza, A. (2000). Postmodern solutions and the limit-opportunity dialectic: The challenge of female penetration and male receptivity. *Gender and Psychoanalysis*, 5:347-357.

Celenza, A. (2005). Vis-à-vis the couch. *International Journal Psyschoanalysis*, 86(6), 1645–1659.

Celenza, A. (2006a). The threat of male to female erotic transference. *Journal American Psychoanalytic Association*, 54(4), 1207–1232.

Celenza, A. (2006b). Hyperconfidentiality and the illusion of the dyad. Paper presented at the *Philadelphia Psychoanalytic Society and Institute*, Philadelphia, PA.

Celenza, A. (2007). *Sexual Boundary Violations: Therapeutic, Supervisory and Academic Contexts*. New York: Jason Aronson.

Celenza, A. (2010). The guilty pleasure of erotic countertransference: Searching for radial true. *Studies in Gender and Sexuality*, 11(4), 175–183.

Celenza, A. (2011). Touching the patient. In S. Akhtar (Ed.), *Unusual Interventions: Alternations of the Frame, Method, and Relationship in Psychotherapy and Psychoanalysis* (pp. 165–176). London: Karnac.

Celenza, A. (2012). From binarial constraints to gender multiplicity: Steve Mitchell's contributions to gender and beyond. Paper presented at the *International Association for Psychoanalysis and Psychotherapy*, New York.

Celenza, A. (2014). *Erotic Revelations: Clinical Applications and Perverse Scenarios*. London: Routledge.

Celenza, A. (2016). Different strokes in boundary artistry. Commentary on Cooper's Blurring boundaries or Why do we refer to sexual misconduct with patients as "Boundary Violation." *Psychoanalytic Dialogues*, 26, 215–222.

Celenza, A. (2017). A Teaching Anthology: The Interpersonal Perspective in Psychoanalysis, 1960s–1990s: Rethinking Transference and Countertransference, D.B. Stern and I. Hirsch (Eds.), Routledge, New York, NY, 2017, 310 pages. *Contemporary Psychoanalysis*, 53, 602–607.

Celenza, A. (2021). Shadows that corrupt: Present absences in psychoanalytic process. In C. Levin (Ed.), *Sexual Boundary Trouble in Psychoanalysis: Clinical Perspectives on Muriel Dimen's Concept of the "Primal Crime."* (pp. 77–93). New York: Routledge.

Celenza, A. (2022a). *Transference, Love, Being: Essential Essays from the Field*. London: Routledge.

Celenza, A. (2022b). Maternal erotic transferences and the work of the abject. *Journal American Psychoanalytic Association*, 70(1), 9–38.

Celenza, A. (2022c). Psychoanalysis and #MeToo: Where are we in this movement? *International Journal of Controversial Discussions*, 2(1), 48–71.

Celenza, A. and Gabbard, G.O. (2003). Analysts who commit sexual boundary violations: A lost cause? *Journal American Psychoanalytic Association*, 51(2), 617–636.

Chasseguet-Smirgel, J. (1970). *Female Sexuality: New Psychoanalytic Views*. London: Karnac.

Chasseguet-Smirgel, J. (1976). Freud and female sexuality: The consideration of some blind spots in the exploration of the 'dark continent.' *International Journal Psychoanalysis*, 57, 275–286.

Chasseguet-Smirgel, J. (1984). *Creativity and Perversion*. New York: Norton.

Chasseguet-Smirgel, J. (1999). Oedipus and psyche. *British Journal Psychotherapy*, 15, 465–475.

Chetrit-Vatine, V. (2004). Primal seduction, matricial space and asymmetry in the psychoanalytic encounter. *International Journal Psychoanalysis*, 85(4), 841–856.

Chodorow, N.J. (2011). *Individualizing Gender and Sexuality: Theory and Practice*. New York: Routledge.

Coen, S. (1992). *The Misuse of Persons: Analyzing Pathological Dependency*. Hillsdale: The Analytic Press.

Coen, S. (1994). Barriers to love between patient and analyst. *Journal American Psychoanalytic Association*, 42, 1107–1135.

Coen, S. (1998). Perverse defenses in neurotic patients. *Journal American Psychoanalytic Association*, 46, 1169–1194.

Cooper, S.H. (1998). Flirting, post-Oedipus, and mutual protectiveness in the analytic dyad: Commentary on paper by Jody Messler Davies. *Psychoanalytic Dialogues*, 8, 767–779.

Cornell, W.F. (2008). Self in action: The bodily basis of self-organization. In F. Sommer Anderson (Ed.), *Bodies in Treatment: The Unspoken Dimension* (pp. 51–76). New York: The Analytic Press.

Davies, J.M. (1994). Love in the afternoon: A relational reconsideration of desire and dread in the countertransference. *Psychoanalytic Dialogues*, 4, 153–170.

Davies, J.M. (1998a). Between the disclosure and foreclosure of erotic transference-countertransference: Can psychoanalysis find a place for adult sexuality? *Psychoanalytic Dialogues*, 8, 747–766.

Davies, J.M. (1998b). Thoughts on the nature of desires: The ambiguous, the transitional, and the poetic. Reply to commentaries. *Psychoanalytic Dialogues*, 8, 805–823.

Davies, J.M. (2001). Erotic overstimulation and the co-construction of sexual meanings in transference-countertransference experience. *Psychoanalytic Quarterly*, 70, 757–788.

de Masi, F. (2012). The erotic transference: Dream or delusion? *Journal American Psychoanalytic Association*, 60, 1199–1220.

de Peyer, J. (2002). Private terrors: Sexualized aggression and a psychoanalyst's fear of her patient. *Psychoanalytic Dialogues*, 12, 509–530.

de Peyer, J. (2022). Unspoken rhapsody: Female erotic countertransference and the dissociation of desire. *Psychoanalytic Perspectives*, 19, 1–19.

de Sade, M. (1785/2013). *The 120 Days of Sadom*. New York: Wilder.

Deutsch, H. (1942). Some forms of emotional disturbance and their relationship to schizophrenia. *Psychoanalytic Quarterly*, 11, 301–321.

Dimen, M. (1991). Deconstructing difference: Gender, splitting, and transitional space. *Psychoanalytic Dialogues*, 1, 335–352.

Dimen, M. (1999). Between lust and libido: Sex psychoanalysis and the moment before. *Psychoanalytic Dialogues*, 9, 415–440.

Dimen, M. (2003). *Sexuality, Intimacy, Power*. Hillsdale, NJ: Analytic Press.

Dimen, M. (2021). Rotten apples and ambivalence: Sexual boundary violations through a psychocultural lens. In C. Levin (Ed.), *Social Aspects of Sexual Boundary Trouble in Psychoanalysis: Responses to the Work of Muriel Dimen* (pp. 29–42). New York: Routledge.

Ehrenberg, D.B. (1992). *The Intimate Edge: Extending the Reach of Psychoanalytic Interaction*. New York: W. W. Norton.

Eidelberg, L. (1948). *Studies in Psychoanalysis*. New York: International University Press.

Elise, D. (1998). Gender repertoire: Body, mind and bisexuality. *Psychoanalytic Dialogues*, 8, 353–372.

Elise, D. (2002). The primary maternal oedipal situation and female homoerotic desire. *Psychoanalytic Inquiry*, 22, 209–228.

Elise, D. (2015). Eroticism in the maternal matrix: Infusion through development and the clinical situation. *Fort Da*, 21(2), 17–32.

Elise, D. (2017). Moving from within the maternal: The choreography of analytic eroticism. *Journal American Psychoanalytic Association*, 65(1), 33–60.

Elise, D. (2019). *Creativity and the Erotic Dimensions of the Analytic Field*. New York: Routledge.

Elise, D. (2020). "Selling fire to the devil": Commentary on Danielle Knafo's "The Sexual Illusionist." *Psychoanalytic Perspectives*, 17, 31–40.

Epstein, R.S., Simon, R.L., and Kay, G.G. (1992). Assessing boundary violations in psychotherapy: Survey results with the Exploitation Index. *Bulletin Menninger Clinic*, 56, 150–166.

Eyman, J.R. and Gabbard, G.O. (1991). Will therapist-patient sex prevent suicide? *Psychiatric Annals*, 21, 669–674.

Faulkner, W. (1951). *Requiem for a Nun*. New York: Random House.

Federn, P. (1952). *Ego Psychology and the Psychoses*. London: Imago.

Fenichel, O. (1937). The scopophilic instinct and identification. *International Journal Psychoanalysis*, 18, 6–34.

Ferenczi, S. (1932a). The language of the unconscious. In *Final Contributions to the Problems and Methods of Psycho-Analysis (Maresfield Library)* (pp. 265–266). London: Hogarth Press.

Ferenczi, S. (1932b). Suppression of the idea of the 'grotesque.' In *Final Contributions to the Problems and Methods of Psycho-Analysis (Maresfield Library)* (pp. 267–268). London: Hogarth Press.

Ferro, A. (1999). *The Bi-Personal Field: Experiences in Child Analysis*. London: Routledge.

Fonagy, P. (2008). A genuinely developmental theory of sexual enjoyment and its implications for psychoanalytic technique. *Journal American Psychoanalytic Association*, 56, 11–36.

Fonagy, P. and Target, M. (2007). The rooting of the mind in the body: New links between attachment theory and psychoanalytic thought. *Journal American Psychoanalytic Association*, 55, 411–456.

Freud, S. (1905). Three essays on the theory of sexuality. *S.E.*, VII (1901–1905), 123–246.

Freud, S. (1910). Wild psychoanalysis. *S.E.*, 11, 219–228.

Freud, S. (1915a). Observations on transference love. *S.E.*, XII, 157–171.

Freud, S. (1915b). Instincts and their vicissitudes. *S.E.*, 14, 109–140.

Freud, S. (1917). Mourning and melancholia. *S.E.*, XIV, 237–258.

Freud, S. (1920). Beyond the pleasure principle. *S.E.*, 18, 1–64.

Freud, S. (1931). Female sexuality. *S.E.*, 21, 223–246.

Gabbard, G.O. (1994a). Of love and lust in erotic transference. *Journal American Psychoanalytic Association*, 42, 385–403.

Gabbard, G.O. (1994b). Psychotherapists who transgress sexual boundaries with patients. *Bulletin Menninger Clinic*, 58(1), 124–135.

Gabbard, G.O. (1996). The analyst's contribution to the erotic transference. *Contemporary Psychoanalysis*, 32, 249.

Gabbard, G.O. (1998). Commentary on paper by Jody Messler Davies. *Psychoanalytic Dialogues*, 8, 781–789.

Gabbard, G.O. (2003). Miscarriages of psychoanalytic treatment with suicidal patients. *International Journal Psychoanalysis*, 84, 249–261.

Gabbard, G.O. (2016). *Boundaries and Boundary Violations in Psychoanalysis*. New York: American Psychiatric Publishing.

Gabbard, G.O. and Lester, E. (1995). Institutional responses. In *Boundaries and Boundary Violations in Psychoanalysis* (pp. 175–195). New York: Basic.

Gabbard, G.O., Peltz, M.L., and COPE Study Group on Boundary Violations (2001). Committee on Psychoanalytic Education: Speaking the unspeakable: Institutional reactions to boundary violations by training analysts. *Journal American Psychoanalytic Association*, 49(2), 659–673.

Gaddini, E. (1969). On imitation. *International Journal Psychoanalysis*, 50, 475–484.

Garrett, T. and Davis, J. (1998). The prevalence of sexual contact between British clinical psychologists and their patients. *Clinical Psychology and Psychotherapy*, 5, 253–256.

Gartrell, N., Herman, J., Olarte, S., Feldstein, M., and Localio, R. (1986). Psychiatrist-patient sexual contact: Results of a national survey, I: Prevalence. *American Journal Psychiatry*, 143(9), 1126–1131.

Gechtman, L. and Bouhoutsos, J. (1985). Sexual intimacy between social workers and clients. Paper presented at the annual meeting of the *Society for Clinical Social Workers*, Universal City, CA.

Gentile, J. (2013). From *Truth or Dare* to *Show and Tell*: Reflections on childhood ritual, play and the evolution of symbolic life. *Psychoanalytic Dialogues*, 23, 150–169.

Gentile, K. (2021). When the cat guards the canary: Using bystander intervention towards community-based response. In C. Levin (Ed.). Sexual Boundary Trouble in Psychoanalysis: Clinical Perspectives on Muriel Dimen's Concept of the "Primal Crime." (pp. 77–100). New York: Routledge.

Goldner, V. (1991). Toward a critical relational theory of gender. *Psychoanalytic Dialogues*, 1, 249–272.

Gonsiorek, J. (1989). Sexual exploitation by psychotherapists: Some observations on male victims and sexual orientation issues. In G. Schoener, J.H. Milgrom, J.C. Gonsiorek, E.T. Luepker and R.M. Conroe (Eds.), *Psychotherapists' Sexual Involvement with Clients: Intervention and Prevention* (pp. 113–119). Minneapolis, MN: Walk-In Counseling Center.

Gonsiorek, J. and Schoener, G.R. (1987). Assessment and evaluation of therapists who sexually exploit clients. *Professional Practice Psychology*, 8(2), 79–93.

Goldner, V. (1991). Toward a critical relational theory of gender. *Psychoanalytic Dialogues*, 1, 249–272.

Green, A. (1986). *On Private Madness*. London: Hogarth Press.

Green, A. (1995). Has sexuality anything to do with psychoanalysis? *International Journal Psychoanalysis*, 76, 871–883.

Green, A. (1999). *The Work of the Negative*. London: Karnac.

Greenacre, P. (1958). Toward an understanding of the physical nucleus of some defence reactions. *International Journal Psychoanalysis*, 39, 69–76.

Greenberg, J. (1999). Analytic authority and analytic restraint. *Contemporary Psychoanalysis*, 35, 25–41.

Greenson, R.R. (1966). A transvestite boy and a hypothesis. *International Journal Psychoanalysis*, 47, 396–403.

Gutheil, T.G. and Gabbard, G.O. (1992). Obstacles to the dynamic understanding of therapist-patient sexual relations. *American Journal Psychotherapy*, 46, 515–526.

Gutheil, T.G. and Gabbard, G.O. (1993). The concept of boundaries in clinical practice: Theoretical and risk management dimensions. *American Journal Psychiatry*, 150, 188–196.

Gutheil, T.G. and Gabbard, G.O. (1998). Misuses and misunderstandings of boundary theory in clinical and regulatory settings. *American Journal Psychiatry*, 155, 409–414.

Hanly, C.M.T. (2004). The third: A brief historical analysis of an idea. *Psychoanalalytic Quarterly*, LXXIII, 267–290.

Harkless, L. (2023). On becoming and being a subject of sexual desire. *Journal American Psychoanalytic Association*, 71(3), 385–418.

Harris, A. (2005). *Gender as Soft Assembly.* Hillsdale, NJ: The Analytic Press.

Harris, A. (2008). The analyst's melancholy and the analyst's omnipotence. Paper presented at the *Boston Psychoanalytic Society and Institute*, Boston, MA.

Hilferding, D. (1911/1974). Zur Grundlage der Mutterliebe. In *Protokolle der Wiener Psychoanalytischen Vereinigung III* (pp. 113–124). Frankfurt: Fischer, 1979. (On the basis of mother-love.) In (1974) *Minutes of the Vienna Psychoanalytic Society, III* (pp. 112–125). New York: International Universities Press, 1974.

Hirsch, I. (1994). Countertransference love and theoretical model. *Psychoanalytic Dialogues*, 4, 171–192.

Hirsch, I. (2008). *Coasting in the Countertransference: Conflicts of Self-Interest between Analyst and Patient.* New York: Routledge.

Hoffer, A. (1996). Asymmetry and mutuality in the analytic relationship: Contemporary lessons from the Freud-Ferenczi dialogue. In P.L. Rudnytsky, A. Bokay and P. Giampieri-Deutsch (Eds.), *Ferenczi's Turn in Psychoanalysis* (pp. 107–119). New York: New York University Press.

Hoffman, I.Z. (1998). Poetic transformations of erotic experience: Commentary on paper by Jody Messler Davies. *Psychoanalytic Dialogues*, 8, 791–804.

Hoffman, I.Z. (2009). Therapeutic passion in the countertransference. *Psychoanalytic Dialogues*, 19, 617–637.

Holroyd, J.C. and Brodsky, A.M. (1977). Psychologists' attitudes and practices regarding erotic and nonerotic physical contact with patients. *American Psychologist*, 32, 843–849.

Horney, K. (1933). The denial of the vagina—A contribution to the problem of the genital anxieties specific to women. *International Journal Psychoanalysis*, 14, 57–70.

Jackson, H. and Nuttall, R.L. (2001). A relationship between childhood sexual abuse and professional sexual misconduct. *Professional Psychology: Research and Practice*, 32(2), 200–204.

Kardener, S.H., Fuller, M., and Mensh, I. (1973). A survey of physicians' attitudes and practices regarding erotic and non-erotic contact with clients. *American Journal Psychiatry*, 130, 1077–1081.

Kernberg, O.F. (1994). Love in the analytic setting. *Journal American Psychoanalytic Association*, 42, 1137–1157.

Kerr, J. (1993). *A Most Dangerous Method: The Story of Jung, Freud, and Sabina Spielrein.* New York: Vintage.

Klein, M. (1930). The importance of symbol formation in the development of the ego. In J. Mitchell (Ed.), *The Selected Melanie Klein* (pp. 95–114). New York: Free Press, 1986.

Knoblauch, S.H. (1995). To speak or not to speak? How and when is that the question?: Commentary on papers by Davies and Gabbard. *Psychoanalytic Dialogues*, 5, 151–155.

Kohut, H. (1977). *The Restoration of the Self*. New York: International University Press.

Kristeva, J. (1980). *Powers of Horror: An Essay on Abjection*. Trans. L.S. Roudiez. New York: Columbia Universities Press.

Kristeva, J. (2000). From symbols to flesh: The polymorphous destiny of narration. *International Journal Psychoanalysis*, 81(4), 771–787.

Kristeva, J. (2011). La reliance, ou de l'érotisme maternal. Available from http://www.kristeva.fr/reliance_film_galabov.html.

Kristeva, J. (2014a). Reliance, or maternal eroticism. *Journal American Psychoanalytic Association*, 62(1), 69–86.

Kristeva, J. (2014b). Julia Kristeva comments on the "Maternal Reliance" section in JAPA. *Journal American Psychoanalytic Association*, 62(3), 60–64.

Kristeva, J. (2019). Prelude to an ethics of the feminine. Keynote address presented at the *International Psychoanalytic Association*, London, England.

Kuchuck, S. (2012). Please (don't) want me: The therapeutic action of male sexual desire in the treatment of heterosexual men. *Contemporary Psychoanalysis*, 48, 544–562.

Kulish, N. (1989). Gender and transference: Conversations with female analysts. *Psychoanalytic Psychology*, 6, 59–71.

Lamb, D.H. and Catanzaro, S.J. (1998). Sexual and nonsexual boundary violations involving psychologists, clients, supervisees, and students. *Professional Psychology, Research and Practice*, 29(5), 498–503.

Lamb, D.H., Woodburn, J.R., Lewis, J.T., Strand, K.K., Buchko, K.J., and Kang, J.R. (1994). Sexual and business relationships between therapists and former clients. *Psychotherapy*, 31(2), 270–278.

Laplanche, J. (1989). *New Foundations for Psychoanalysis*. London: Blackwell.

Laplanche, J. (1997). The theory of seduction and the problem of the other. *International Journal Psychoanalysis*, 78, 653–666.

Laplanche, J. (1999). Transference: Its provocation by the analyst. In *Essays on Otherness* (pp. 214–233). London: Routledge.

Laplanche, J. and Pontalis, J.-B. (1973). *The Language of Psychoanalysis*. New York: Norton.

Leavitt, J. (2017). From group-ethic to group-erotic. Paper presented at the *International Psychoanalytic Association*, Buenos Aires, Argentina.

Lester, E. (1985). The female analyst and the erotized transference. *International Journal Psychoanalysis*, 66, 283–293.

Levinas, E. (1961). *Totalité et infini: Essai sur l'extériorité [Totality and infinite: Essays on exteriority]*. Paris: Le Livre de Poche.

Lingiardi, V. (2007). Dreaming gender: Restoration and transformation. *Studies in Gender and Sexuality*, 8, 313–331.

Lijtmaer, R.M. (2004). The place of erotic transference and countertransference in clinical practice. *Journal American Academy Psychoanalysis*, 32, 483–498.

Litowitz, B.E. (2014). Introduction to Julia Kristeva. *Journal American Psychoanalytic Association*, 62(1), 57–60.

Loewald, H. (1970). Psychoanalytic theory and the psychoanalytic process. *Psychoanalytic Study Child*, 25, 45–68.

Lombardi, R. (2016). *Formless Infinity: Clinical Explorations of Matte Blanco and Bion*. London: Routledge.

Long, K.M. (2005). Panel report: The changing language of female development. *Journal American Psychoanalytic Association*, 53(4), 1161–1174.

Makari, G. (2008). *Revolution in Mind: The Creation of Psychoanalysis*. New York: Harper Perennial.

Mann, D. (1994). The psychotherapist's erotic subjectivity. *British Journal Psychotherapy*, 10, 344–354.

McDougall, J. (1986). Identifications, neoneeds and neosexualities. *International Journal Psychoanalysis*, 67, 19–31.

McDougall, J. (1992). *Plea for a Measure of Abnormality*. New York: Brunner/Mazel.

McDougall, J. (1995). *The Many Faces of Eros*. New York: Norton.

Merleau-Ponty, M. (1964/1945). *Signs*. Trans. R.C. McCleary. Evanston, IL: Northwestern University Press.

Merleau-Ponty, M. (2012/1945). *Phenomenology of Perception*. Trans. C. Smith. New York: Routledge.

Modell, A. (1990). Transference and levels of reality. In *Other Times, Other Realities* (pp. 44–59). Cambridge, MA: Harvard University Press.

Modell, A. (1991). Resistance to the exposure of the private self. *Contemporary Psychoanalysis*, 27, 731–736.

Morris, H. (2012). Constituting the ethics of psychoanalysis: Observations on "Observations on Transference Love," the story. Paper presented on Panel on Ethics, *Boston Psychoanalytic Society and Institute*, May 2012.

Moya, P. and Larrain, M.W. (2016). Sexuality and meaning in Freud and Merleau-Ponty. *International Journal Psychoanalysis*, 97(3), 737–757.

Myerson, P.G. (1969). The hysteric's experience in psychoanalysis. *International Journal Psychoanalysis*, 50, 373–384.

Ogden, T. (1994). *Subjects of Analysis*. Northvale, NJ: Jason Aronson.

Parsons, J.P. and Wincze, J.P. (1995). A survey of client-therapist sexual involvement in Rhode Island as reported by subsequent treating therapists. *Professional Psychology: Research and Practice*, 26, 171–175.

Perelberg, R.J. (2018). Introduction: A psychoanalytic understanding of psychic bisexuality. In R.J. Perelberg (Ed.), *Psychic Bisexuality* (pp. 1–57). London: Routledge.

Person, E.S. (1985). The erotic transference in women and men: Differences and consequences. *Journal of the American Psychoanalytic Association*, 13, 159–180.

Plakun, E. (1999). Sexual misconduct and enactment. *Journal Psychotherapy, Practice and Research*, 8(4), 284–291.

Pope, K.S. and Bouhoutsos, J.C. (1986). *Sexual Intimacy between Therapists and Patients*. New York: Praeger.

Pope, K.S., Levenson, H., and Schover, L.R. (1979). Sexual intimacy in psychology training: Results and implications of a national survey. *American Psychologist*, 34, 682–689.

Pope, K.S., Keith-Spiegel, P., and Tabachnick, B.G. (1986). Sexual attraction to clients: The human therapist and the (sometimes) inhuman training system. *American Psychologist*, 41, 147–158.

Pope, K.S., Tabachnick, B.G., and Keith-Spiegel, P. (1987). Ethics of practice: The beliefs and behaviors of psychologists as therapists. *American Psychologist*, 42, 993–1006.

Renik, O. (1993). Analytic interaction: Conceptualizing technique in the light of the analyst's irreducible subjectivity. *Psychoanalytic Quarterly*, 62, 553–571.

Renik, O. (1999). Playing one's cards face up analysis: An approach to the problem of self-disclosure. *Psychoanalytic Quarterly*, 68, 521–539.

Renn, P. (2013). Moments of meeting: The relational challenges of sexuality in the consulting room. *British Journal Psychotherapy*, 29, 135–153.

Rilke, R.M. (1939). *Duino Elegies*. Trans. J.B. Leishman and S. Spender. New York: Norton, 1963.

Ritvo, S., and Provence, S. (1953). Form perception and imitation in some autistic children: Diagnostic findings and their contextual interpretation. *Psychoanalytic Study Child*, 8, 155–161.

Rodolfa, E., Hall, T., Holms, V., Davena, A., Komatz, D., Antunez, M., and Hall, A. (1994). The management of sexual feeings in therapy. *Professional Psychology: Research and Practice*, 25(2), 168–172.

Saketopoulou, A. (2019). The draw to overwhelm: Consent, risk, and the retranslation of enigma. *Journal American Psychoanalytic Association*, 67(1), 133–167.

Saketopoulou, A. (2020). The infantile erotic countertransference: The analyst's infantile sexual, ethics and the role of the psychoanalytic collective. *Psychoanalytic Inquiry*, 40(8), 659–677.

Saketopoulou, A. (2021). Does sexuality have anything to do with sexual boundary violations? In C. Levin (Ed.), *Sexual Boundary Trouble in Psychoanalysis: Clinical Perspectives on Muriel Dimen's Concept of the "Primal Crime"* (pp. 101–128). New York: Routledge.

Saketopoulou, A. and Pellegrini, A. (2023). *Gender Without Identity*. New York: The Unconscious in Translation.

Salomonsson, B. (2012). Has infantile sexuality anything to do with infants? *International Journal Psychoanalysis*, 93(3), 631–647.

Samuels, A. (1985). Symbolic dimensions of eros in transference-counter transference: Some clinical uses of Jung's alchemical metaphor. *International Review of Psychoanalysis*, 12, 199–214.

Samuels, A. (1996). From sexual misconduct to social justice. *Psychoanalytic Dialogues*, 6, 295–321.

Sandler, A.-M. (2004). Institutional responses to boundary violations: The case of Masud Khan. *Internationall Journal Psychoanalysis*, 85, 27–42.

Scarfone, D. (2015). *The Unpast*. New York: The Unconscious in Translation.

Scarfone, D. (2023). *The Reality of the Message: Psychoanalysis in the Wake of Jean Laplanche*. New York: The Unconscious in Translation.

Schafer, R. (1968). *Aspects of Internalization*. New York: International Universities Press.

Schiller, B.M. (2012). Representing female desire within a labial framework of sexuality. *Journal American Psychoanalytic Association*, 60, 1161–1197.

Schoener, G. and Gonsiorek, J. (1989). Assessment and development of rehabilitation plans for the therapist. In G.R. Schoener, Milgrom, J.H., Gonsiorek, J.C., Luepker, E.T., and Conroe, R.M. (Eds.), *Psychotherapists' Sexual Involvement with Clients: Intervention and Prevention* (pp. 401–420). Minneapolis, MN: Walk-In Counseling Center.

Schoener, G.R., Milgrom, J.H., Gonsiorek, J.C., Luepker, E.T., and Conroe, R.M. (Eds.) (1989). *Psychotherapists' Sexual Involvement with Clients: Intervention and Prevention* (pp. 399–502). Minneapolis, MN: Walk-In Counseling Center.

Schore, A.N. (2011). The right brain implicit self lies at the core of psychoanalysis. *Psychoanalytic Dialogues*, 21, 75–100.

Searles, H.F. (1979). *Countertransference and Related Subjects: Selected Papers*. Madison, CT: International Universities Press.

Shakespeare, W. (2000). Sonnet 23. In S. Booth (Ed.), *Shakespeare's Sonnets*. New Haven, CT: Yale Nota Bene, Yale University Press.

Slavin, J.H., Rahmani, M., and Pollock, L. (1998). Reality and danger in psychoanalytic treatment. *Psychoanalytic Quarterly*, 67, 191–217.

Slavin, J.H. (2013). Moments of truth and perverse scenarios in psychoanalysis: Revisiting Davies' "Love in the afternoon." *Psychoanalytic Dialogues*, 23, 139–149.

Slochower, J. (1999). Erotic complications. *International Journal Psychoanalysis*, 80, 1119–1130.

Slochower, J. (2003). The analyst's secret delinquencies. *Psychoanalytic Dialogues*, 13, 451–469.

Slochower, J. (2015). An erotic dream, an erotic collision. *Annual of Psychoanalysis*, 38, 87–104.

Slochower, J. (2024). *Psychoanalysis and the Unspoken*. London: Routledge.

Smith, S. (1977). The Golden Fantasy: A regressive reaction to separation anxiety. *International Journal Psychoanalysis*, 58, 311–324.

Smith, S. (1984) The sexually abused patient and the abusing therapist: A study in sadomasochistic relationships. *Psychoanalytic Psychology*, 1(2), 89–98.

Somer, E. and Saadon, J. (1999). Therapit-client sex: Clients' restrospective reports. *Professional Psychology: Research and Practice*, 30(5), 504–509.

Spezzano, C. (1998). The triangle of clinical judgment. *Journal American Psychoanalytic Association*, 46, 365–388.

Stake, J.E. and Oliver, J. (1991). Sexual contact and touching between therapist and client: A survey of psychologists' attitudes and behavior. *Professional Psychology: Research and Practice*, 22(4), 297–307.

Stein, R. (1995a). Analysis of a case of transsexualism. *Psychoanalytic Dialogues*, 5, 257–289.

Stein, R. (1995b). Reply to Chodorow. *Psychoanalytic Dialogues*, 5, 301–310.

Stoller, R.J. (1966). The mother's contribution to infantile transvestic behavior. *International Journal Psychoanalysis*, 47, 384–395.

Stoller, R. (1968). *Sex and Gender*. New York: Science House.

Stolorow, R. (1975). The narcissistic function of masochism (and sadism). *International Journal Psychoanalysis*, 56, 441–448.

Stotland, E. (1969). Exploratory investigations of empathy. In L. Berkowitz (Ed.), *Advances in Experimental Social Psychology*, Vol. 4. New York: Academic Press.

Strean, H.S. (1993). *Therapists Who Have Sex with Their Patients: Treatment and Recovery*. New York: Brunner/Mazel.

Theogony of Hesiod [c. 730–700 BC/2018].

Twemlow, S.W. and Gabbard, G.O. (1989). The lovesick therapist. In G.O. Gabbard (Ed.), *Sexual Exploitation in Professional Relationships*. Washington, DC: American Psychiatric Press.

Wheelis, J., Michels, R., Celenza, A., and Gabbard, G.O. (2003). How could this happen to me? Panel on sexual boundary violations among psychoanalysts. *American Psychoanalytic Association*, New York, 2003.

Widawsky, R. (2014). Julia Kristeva's psychoanalytic work. *Journal American Psychoanalytic Association*, 62(1), 61–68.

Wilson, M. (2013). Desire and responsibility: The ethics of countertransference experience. *Psychoanalytic Quarterly*, 82, 435–476.

Wilson, M. (2014). Maternal reliance: Commentary on Kristeva. *Journal American Psychoanalytic Association*, 62(1), 101–111.

Winnicott, D.W. (1960). The theory of the parent-infant relationship. *International Journal Psychoanalysis*, 41, 585–595.

Winnicott, D.W. (1971). *Playing and Reality*. New York: Routledge.

Wrye, H.K. and Welles, J.K. (1994). *The Narration of Desire: Erotic Transferences and Countertransferences*. Hillsdale, NJ: The Analytic Press.

Zeavin, L. (2019). The elusive good object. *Psychoanalytic Quarterly*, 88(1), 75–93.

Index

Printed and bound by CPI Group (UK) Ltd, Croydon, CR0 4YY
08/06/2025
01897000-0004